1 MONTH OF FREE READING

at

www.ForgottenBooks.com

By purchasing this book you are eligible for one month membership to ForgottenBooks.com, giving you unlimited access to our entire collection of over 700,000 titles via our web site and mobile apps.

To claim your free month visit:
www.forgottenbooks.com/free262231

* Offer is valid for 45 days from date of purchase. Terms and conditions apply.

ISBN 978-0-483-81838-5
PIBN 10262231

This book is a reproduction of an important historical work. Forgotten Books uses state-of-the-art technology to digitally reconstruct the work, preserving the original format whilst repairing imperfections present in the aged copy. In rare cases, an imperfection in the original, such as a blemish or missing page, may be replicated in our edition. We do, however, repair the vast majority of imperfections successfully; any imperfections that remain are intentionally left to preserve the state of such historical works.

Forgotten Books is a registered trademark of FB &c Ltd.
Copyright © 2017 FB &c Ltd.
FB &c Ltd, Dalton House, 60 Windsor Avenue, London, SW19 2RR.
Company number 08720141. Registered in England and Wales.

For support please visit www.forgottenbooks.com

CHARTER
FIRE INSURANCE PATROL LAW
PATROLMEN'S PENSION FUND LAW
CONSTITUTION AND BY-LAWS

OF

THE CHICAGO BOARD OF UNDERWRITERS
OF CHICAGO

Revised and Approved February 1, 1882
Amended January 11, 1906

CHICAGO
JACOBS & HOLMES, PRINTERS AND PUBLISHERS
1906

AN ACT

TO INCORPORATE THE CHICAGO BOARD OF UNDERWRITERS OF THE CITY OF CHICAGO.

SECTION 1. Be it enacted by the people of the State of Illinois, represented in the General Assembly, that T. L. Miller, Julius White, H. B. Wilmarth, C. N. Holden, S. T. Atwater, B. W. Phillips, S. C. Higginson, Alfred James and their associates, now composing the Chicago Board of Underwriters, and such parties as may hereafter be admitted members thereof, are hereby created a body politic and corporate, under the name and style of "THE CHICAGO BOARD OF UNDERWRITERS OF CHICAGO"; and by that name may sue and be sued, implead and be impleaded, receive and hold property and effects, real and personal, by gift, devise or purchase, and dispose of the same by sale, lease or otherwise; said property so held not to exceed at any time the sum of two hundred thousand dollars; may have a common seal, and alter the same from time to time, and make such by-laws, rules and regulations, from time to time, as they may think proper or necessary for the government of the corporation and the management of their business and the mode in which it shall be transacted, as they may think proper, not contrary to the laws of the land.

CONSTITUTION AND BY-LAWS.

SEC. 2. That the constitution, by-laws and rules and regulations of the said existing Chicago Board of Underwriters shall be the constitution, by-laws and rules and regulations of the corporation hereby created until the same shall be regularly repealed or altered; and the present officers of the said Board, known as the Chicago Board of Underwriters, shall be the officers of the corporation hereby created, until their respective offices shall regularly expire, or be vacated, and until the election *and installation* of new officers, according to the provisions *hereof.*

OFFICERS.

SEC. 3. The officers shall consist of a President, Vice-President, Treasurer, Secretary and Chief Surveyor, and such other officers as may be determined upon by the by-laws, rules and regulations of said corporation. All of said officers shall, respectively, hold their offices for the length of time fixed upon by the by-laws, rules and regulations of the said corporation hereby created, and until their successors are elected and qualified.

OBJECT.

SEC. 4. The object of this corporation shall be to promote the best interests of all insurance companies transacting the business of marine, fire and life insurance in the State of Illinois.

COMMITTEES.

SEC. 5. Said corporation may elect, constitute and appoint committees of arbitration and appeal, and committees on fines and penalties, who shall be governed by such by-laws, tariffs, and rules and regulations for the settlement of such matters as may be voluntarily or otherwise submitted to them by the corporation. The acting chairman of any committee so elected, constituted or appointed may administer oaths to the parties and witnesses, and issue subpoenas and attachments, compelling the attendance of parties and witnesses the same as a justice of peace, and in like manner directed to any constable to execute.

SURVEYORS AND FIRE WARDENS.

SEC. 6. Said corporation shall have power to elect a Chief Surveyor and to appoint as many Assistant Surveyors as they may see fit, who shall have the legal right to examine, inspect and survey any property whatever, insured, or upon which application is made for insurance, and all property upon which insurance can be effected, and such Surveyors may be appointed and act as Fire Marshals, Fire Police or Fire Wardens, by and under any municipal or State authority, within the State of Illinois, that has the power to appoint them as such.

FINES.

SEC. 7. Said corporation may inflict fines upon any of its members, and collect the same, for breach of its by-laws, rules, regulations, tariffs and rates. Such fines may be collected by action of debt, before a justice of the peace, in the name of the corporation.

POWER OF THE CORPORATION.

SEC. 8. Said corporation shall have no power or authority to do or carry on any business, excepting such as is heretofore mentioned in this act of incorporation, or such as is usual in boards or associations of underwriters.

Approved February 22, 1861.

AN ACT to enable boards of underwriters incorporated by or under the laws of the State of Illinois to establish and maintain a fire patrol.

SECTION 1. Be it enacted by the People of the State of Illinois represented in the General Assembly, that boards of underwriters, incorporated by or under the laws of the State of Illinois, shall have power to provide suitable rooms for the accommodation of a fire patrol, and also to provide a patrol of men and a competent person to act as superintendent to discover and prevent fires, with suitable apparatus to have and preserve property or life at and after a fire, and the better to enable them so to act with promptness and efficiency, full power is given such superintendent and such patrol to enter any building on fire or which may be exposed to or in danger of taking fire from other burning buildings subject to the control of the fire marshal of the city, and at once to proceed to protect and endeavor to save the property therein and to remove such property, or any part thereof, from the ruins after a fire.

SEC. 2. In the month of July of each year there shall be held a meeting of said board of underwriters, of which ten days' previous notice shall be inserted in at least one daily newspaper, published in the city where said board of underwriters is located, at which meeting each insurance company, corporation, association, underwriter, agent, person or persons, doing a fire insurance business in the city, shall have the right to be represented at such meetings and shall be entitled to vote.

A majority of the whole number so represented shall have power to decide upon the question of sustaining the fire patrol hereinbefore mentioned, and of fixing the maximum amount of expenses which shall be incurred therefor during the fiscal year next to ensue, which amount shall in no case exceed two per centum on the aggregate of premiums returned as received, as provided in section three of this act, and the whole of such amount or so much thereof as may be necessary, may be assessed upon all insurance companies, organizations, corporations, associations and persons who assume risks and accept premium for fire insurance in said city as hereinbefore mentioned in proportion to the several amounts of premiums returned as received by each as hereinafter provided, and such assessment shall be collectable by and in the name of said board of underwriters in any Court of Law in the State of Illinois having jurisdiction in such manner and at such time or times as said board of underwriters may determine.

SEC. 3. To provide for the payment of persons employed under the provisions of this act, and to maintain suitable rooms, and the apparatus for saving life and property contemplated, said board of underwriters is empowered to require a statement to be furnished semi-annually by all insurance companies, corporations, associations, underwriters, agents or persons, of the aggregate amount of premiums received for insuring property in the city *where said board of* underwriters is organized or established for

and during the six months next preceding the first day of July and the first day of January of each year, which statement shall be sworn to by the President or Secretary of the corporation or association or by the agent or person so acting and effecting such insurance in said city and shall be handed to the Secretary of said board of underwriters, within such time as is hereinafter provided in section four of this act.

SEC. 4. It shall be lawful for the Secretary or other appointed officer of said board of underwriters, within ten days after the first day of July and first day of January in each year, by written or printed demand, signed by him, to require from every insurance company, corporation, association, underwriter, agent or person engaged in the business of fire insurance in the city where said board of underwriters is organized or established, the statement provided for in the last preceding section of this act. Such demand may be delivered personally at the office of such insurance company, corporation, association, underwriter, agent or person, and every officer of such insurance company, corporation or association and every individual agent, underwriter or person, who shall for fifteen days after such demand neglect to send the account shall forfeit fifty dollars for the use of said board of underwriters, and he shall also forfeit for its use twenty-five dollars in addition, for every day he shall so neglect after the expiration of the said fifteen days; and such additional penalty may be computed and recovered up to the time of trial of any suit for the recovery thereof, which penalty may be sued for and recovered with costs of suit, in any court of law within the State of Illinois, having jurisdiction, by and in the name of said board of underwriters.

      (Signed) S. M. CULLOM,
    Speaker of the House of Representatives.
          JOHN EARLY.
        President of the Senate.

Approved March 28th, 1874.
 JOHN L. BEVERIDGE,
   Governor.

AN ACT to create an organization and a fund for the pensioning of disabled fire insurance patrolmen, and the widows and children of deceased patrolmen, and authorizing the retirement from service and the pensioning of members of the fire insurance patrol in cities, villages and towns where the population exceeds 50,000 inhabitants, having a paid fire insurance patrol.

SECTION 1. Be it enacted by the People of the State of Illinois, represented in the General Assembly, That in all cities, villages or incorporated towns whose population exceeds 50,000, having a paid fire insurance patrol, a fund may be created by the board of underwriters of such cities, villages or towns for the pensioning of disabled fire insurance patrolmen and the widows and children of deceased patrolmen; to authorize the retirement from service and the pensioning of members of the fire insurance patrol, and for other purposes connected therewith. Such fund shall be controlled and managed by a board of trustees composed of the President, Secretary, Treasurer, Chairman of the Patrol Committee, and the Superintendent or chief officers of the fire insurance patrol of the board of underwriters of such city, village or town, under the name of "The Board of Trustees of the Patrolmen's Pension Fund." The said board shall elect from their number a President, Secretary and Treasurer.

SEC. 2. The said board of trustees shall have exclusive control and management of all money donated, paid or assessed for the relief or pensioning disabled, superannuated and retired members of the fire insurance patrol, their widows and minor children, and shall assess each member of the fire insurance patrol not to exceed one per cent of the salary of such member to be deducted and withheld from the monthly pay of each member so assessed. And the Treasurer of the board of underwriters of such city, village or town shall set aside and pay to the Treasurer of said board of trustees not to exceed two per cent of all moneys paid to him by insurance companies for the support of said fire insurance patrol, the same to be placed by the Treasurer of said board of trustees to the credit of such fund subject to the order of such board of trustees.

The said board shall make all needful rules and regulations for its government in the discharge of its duties; shall hear and decide all applications for relief or pensions under this act and its decisions on such applications shall be final and conclusive and not subject to review or reversal except by the board of trustees. The said board of trustees shall cause to be kept a record of all its meetings and proceedings.

SEC. 3. All rewards in moneys, fees, gifts and emoluments that shall be paid or given for or on account of extraordinary services by said fire insurance patrol or any member thereof (except when allowed to be retained by such member, or given to endow a medal or other permanent or competitive award) shall be paid into said pension fund.

Sec. 4. The said board of trustees may invest such funds or any part thereof in the name of the board of trustees of the patrolmen's pension fund in such interest bearing securities as may be approved by the said board of trustees, and all such securities shall be deposited with the Treasurer and shall be subject to the order of said board of trustees.

Sec. 5. If any member of the fire insurance patrol of such city, village or town shall, while in the performance of his duty, become and be found upon examination by a medical officer, ordered by said board of trustees, to be physically or mentally permanently disabled by reason of service in such department so as to render necessary his retirement from service in said fire insurance patrol, said board of trustees shall retire such member from service in such fire insurance patrol. Upon such retirement, the said board of trustees shall order the payment to said disabled member of said fire insurance patrol, monthly, from such pension fund a sum equal to one-half of the monthly compensation allowed to such member as salary at the date of his retirement.

Sec. 6. If any member of such fire insurance patrol shall, while in the performance of his duty, be killed or die as the result of an injury received in the line of his duty, or of any disease contracted by reason of his occupation, or if any member of such fire insurance patrol shall die from any cause while in said service, or during retirement, or after retirement, after twenty-two years' service, as hereinafter provided, and shall leave a widow, or children under sixteen years of age surviving, said board of trustees shall direct the payment from said pension fund of the following sum monthly, to-wit: to such widow while unmarried, $30.00; to the guardian of such minor child or children, $6.00 for each of said children until it or they reach the age of sixteen years: Provided, that there shall not be paid to a family of a deceased member a total pension exceeding one-half the monthly salary of said deceased member at the time of his decease, or, if a retired member, a sum not exceeding one-half the amount of the monthly salary of such retired member at the date of his retirement.

If at any time there shall not be sufficient money in such pension fund to pay each person entitled to the benefits thereof the full amount per month as hereinbefore provided, then, and in that event, an equal percentage of such monthly payments shall be made to each beneficiary thereof until the said fund shall be replenished to warrant the payment in full to each of said persons.

Sec. 7. Any member of the fire insurance patrol of any city, village or town, after becoming fifty years of age and having served twenty-two years or more in such fire insurance patrol, of which the last two years shall be continuous, may make application to be relieved from such fire insurance patrol, or if he shall be discharged from such fire insurance patrol the said board of trustees shall order and direct that such person shall

be paid a monthly pension equal to one-half the amount of salary attached to the rank which he may have held in said fire insurance patrol at the date of his retirement or discharge. And the said board, upon the recommendation of the superintendent or chief officer of the patrol provided for in this act, shall have the power to assign members of the fire insurance patrol, retired or drawing pensions under this act, to the performance of light duties in said fire insurance patrol. After the decease of such member, his widow, or minor child or children under sixteen years of age, if any surviving, shall be entitled to the pension provided for in this act. But nothing in this or any other section of this act shall warrant the payment of any annuity to any widow of a deceased member of such fire insurance patrol after she shall have remarried.

SEC. 8. This act shall apply to all persons who are now or shall hereafter become members of such fire insurance patrol and all such persons shall be eligible to the benefits secured by this act.

SEC. 9. The Treasurer of the board of trustees shall be the custodian of said pension fund and shall secure and safely keep the same subject to the control and direction of the board, and shall keep his books and accounts concerning said fund in such manner as shall be prescribed by the board of trustees; and the said books and accounts shall always be subject to the inspection of the board of trustees or any member thereof. The Treasurer shall within ten days after his election or appointment, execute a bond to the board of underwriters with good and sufficient security in such penal sum as the board shall direct, to be approved by the board of trustees. Conditions, for the faithful performance of the duties of his office and that he will safely keep, hold and truly account for all moneys and property which may come into his hands as such Treasurer and that upon the expiration of his term of office he will surrender and turn over to his successor all unexpended moneys and all property which may have come into his hands as Treasurer of such fund. Such bond shall be filed in the office of the board of underwriters, and in case of a breach of the same or the conditions thereof suit may be brought on the same in the name of such board of underwriters for the use of such board or of any person or persons injured by such breach.

SEC. 10. All moneys ordered to be paid from said pension fund to any person or persons shall be paid by the Treasurer of said board only upon warrants signed by the President of the board and countersigned by the Secretary thereof, and no warrant shall be drawn except by order of the board of trustees and duly entered in the records of the proceedings of the board. In case the said pension fund or any part thereof shall by order of said board of trustees or otherwise be deposited in any bank or loaned, all interest on money which may be paid or agreed to be paid on account of any such loan or deposit shall belong to and constitute a part of such fund: Provided, that nothing

herein contained shall be construed as authorizing said Treasurer to loan or deposit such fund or any part of such fund unless so authorized by the board of trustees.

SEC. 11. The board of trustees shall make report to the board of underwriters of such city, village or town of the condition of such pension fund on the first day of January of each and every year.

SEC. 12. No portion of said pension fund shall either before or after its order of distribution by such board to such disabled members of said fire insurance patrol or to the widow or guardian of such minor child or children of deceased or retired member of such fire insurance patrol be held, seized, taken, subjected to, or detained, or levied on by virtue of any attachment, execution, injunction, writ, interlocutory, or other order or decree, or any process or proceeding whatever issued of or by any court of this State for the payment or satisfaction in whole or in part of any debt, damages, claim, demand, or judgment against such member or his widow or the guardian of said minor child or children of any deceased member, but the said fund shall be sacredly held, kept secure and distributed for the purpose of pensioning the persons named in this act and for no other purpose whatever.

     (Signed) JOHN MEYER,
        Speaker of the House.
       JOSEPH B. GILL,
        President of the Senate.

Approved June 24th, 1895.
 (Signed) JOHN P. ALTGELD,
     Governor.

CONSTITUTION

ARTICLE I.
TITLE.
Principal Office.

Name   1   This corporation shall be called by its corporate name, "The
2 Chicago Board of Underwriters of Chicago," and its principal
Office   3 office and place of business shall be in the city of Chicago, Illi-
4 nois, but it may maintain branch offices or places of business
5 elsewhere in the State of Illinois.

ARTICLE II.
OBJECT.

Object   6   "The object of this corporation shall be to promote the best
7 interests of all insurance companies transacting the business of
8 marine, fire and life insurance in the State of Illinois" under
9 the authority thereof, particularly by encouraging the construc-
Inspection   10 tion of good buildings, by maintaining a system of inspection of
11 same and of the equipment and occupancy thereof, whereby the
12 danger of fires happening may be reduced, by encouraging effi-
Fire Protection   13 cient public and private fire protection and the maintenance of a
14 fire patrol, whereby the destruction of life and property may be
15 lessened, by establishing and encouraging good practices in un-
Underwriting   16 derwriting, whereby the insuring public may be furnished con-
17 current policies of insurance by companies duly authorized by
18 the State of Illinois, by adopting equitable tariffs, rates and rules,
Losses by Fire   19 whereby the losses of the insured by fire may be fairly distributed
20 among the insured according to risk and value of destructible or
21 damageable property, by discouraging extravagant expenditure
Expenses   22 in the conduct of the business, whereby the expense of protec-
23 tion to the insured may not be made unreasonable, by encour-
Arson   24 aging the discovery and punishment of the crime of arson,
25 whereby the destruction by fire of property with fraudulent or
26 malicious intent with its attendant danger to life may be checked,
27 and by creating a fund in compliance with the law with which
Pension   28 to pension disabled and retired patrolmen, and the widows and
29 children of such as are deceased, whereby the performance of
30 duty in saving life and property in a service of so perilous a na-
31 ture may be substantially recognized.

ARTICLE III.
POWERS.

Limit of Government   32   The corporation shall not assume power or authority to do
33 or carry on any business excepting such as is provided for in its
34 charter, or under a general law, and such as is usual in boards
35 or associations of underwriters.

ARTICLE IV.

TERRITORIAL SUB-DIVISIONS OF COOK COUNTY.

Districts   1   The natural areas of operations of members are defined as 2 the central office district, the principal city district, the suburban 3 city district, and the county district.

Central Office   4   The *Central Office District* is that territory in the City of 5 Chicago bounded on the north by the Chicago River, on the 6 east by Lake Michigan, on the south by Harrison street, and on 7 the west by the south branch of the Chicago River.

Principal City   8   The *Principal City District* is that territory in the city of 9 Chicago (including the central office district) within the follow- 10 ing boundary lines: Beginning at the intersection of Fullerton 11 avenue with the Chicago River, thence east to Lake Michigan, 12 thence southerly to Oakwood avenue, thence west to Ellis ave- 13 nue, thence north to Thirty-ninth street, thence west to Halsted 14 street, thence south to Forty-seventh street, thence west to Loo- 15 mis street, thence north to Forty-fifth street, thence west to Ash- 16 land avenue, thence north to Thirty-ninth street, thence west 17 to Western avenue, thence north to Illinois and Michigan Canal, 18 thence westerly to West Fortieth avenue, thence north to West 19 North avenue, thence east to Northwestern avenue, thence north 20 to Belmont avenue, thence southerly along the north branch of 21 the Chicago River to Fullerton avenue, at the place of begin- 22 ning.

Suburban City   23   The *Suburban City District* is all that territory outside of 24 the principal city district as is within the limits of the City of 25 Chicago as now or hereafter constituted.

County   26   The *County District* is all that part of Cook County, Illinois, 27 lying and being outside of the City of Chicago as now or here- 28 after constituted.

ARTICLE V.

MEMBERSHIPS.

Memberships   29   Memberships in the corporation are personal privileges, to be 30 enjoyed by those admitted thereto during such time as they 31 remain qualified therefor and abide by their membership agree- 32 ment.

Qualifications   33   Natural persons, or firms, each and every one of the partners 34 of which are and remain qualified therefor engaged in the 35 business of insurance, may be admitted to membership in the 36 appropriate class hereinafter provided, according to the degree 37 of authority (if any) held by them from a fire insurance com- 38 pany authorized to do business in the State of Illinois, to the 39 manner in which such company transacts its business, to the 40 territory in which the member would naturally operate, to the 41 location of his office, to other kinds of business in which he may 42 be engaged, to the manner in which he conducts his business.

MEMBERSHIP—CLASS ONE.

Class One   43   Natural persons or firms principally engaged in the business

of insurance may be admitted to membership in Class One of the corporation if engaged in such business in the capacity and manner hereinafter set forth: Either as

Officer
An officer of a fire insurance company; or
Where such company has no officer holding a membership then as the manager or general agent of a fire insurance company, having superior and exclusive jurisdiction for such company in all matters over the entire County of Cook; or

Agent
An agent of a fire insurance company having authority from the company to make and execute policies of insurance covering property wherever situate in the County of Cook, and each subject to the following qualifications.

Office
Where the person or firm maintains but one office for the transaction of local insurance business, and such office is located in the central office district described.

Company Representation
Where the person or firm represents only such insurance companies as are duly admitted to the State of Illinois and comply with the laws thereof, and where such company has no more than three agents or agencies, having offices within the central office district described, for the transaction of local business, and none elsewhere, authorized to make and execute contracts of insurance covering property situate in what is described as the principal city district.

Where the person or firm only represents such fire insurance companies, as confine their representation in Cook County to members of this corporation.

Observance of Rules
Where the applicant agrees to abide by, observe and uphold the constitution, by-laws, rules, regulations, tariffs and rates of the corporation, as now or hereafter made and to enforce compliance therewith by all agents or others under his or their jurisdiction, if recommended by a majority vote of the Executive Committee, and if three-fifths (3-5) of the total vote held by the membership are cast in favor of admitting the applicant.

MEMBERSHIP—CLASS TWO.

Class Two
Natural persons, or firms, whose exclusive business is insurance, or insurance with banking, real estate and loans, whose sole place of business is in the suburban city district described, and persons or firms, whose place of business and entire business of every nature is located in the county district, and who, in each case, also represent only such fire insurance company or companies over the affairs of which a member of Class One of this corporation has superior and exclusive jurisdiction in the entire county of Cook, and whose authority as agent for such company or companies does not cover the territory comprised within the principal city district, may be admitted to membership in Class Two of the corporation, if recommended by two officials of the corporation, and elected by the Executive Committee of the corporation.

12

MEMBERSHIP—CLASS THREE.

Class Three. 1 The following described natural persons or firms may be 2 admitted to membership in Class Three upon recommendation of 3 two officials of the corporation, if elected by the Executive Com- 4 mittee.

Business. 5 If they are exclusively engaged in the business of insurance.

Office. 6 If their sole office or place of business being located in the 7 County of Cook outside of the central office district described, 8 they are exclusively engaged in insurance together with bank- 9 ing, buying, selling or renting real estate for others, and—or 10 lending money on real estate for others.

Company Representation. 11 If they do not represent any fire insurance company in any 12 capacity.

Dues. 13 If they pay annual dues of ten dollars to the corporation.

MEMBERSHIP—CLASS FOUR.

Class Four. 14 The following described natural persons or firms may be 15 admitted to membership in Class Four upon the recommenda- 16 tion of two officials of the corporation: 17 If elected by the Executive Committee.

Business. 18 If they are principally engaged in the business of buying, 19 selling and—or renting real estate for others, or lending money 20 on real estate for others.

Office. 21 If their principal office is located within the central office 22 district described.

Company Representation. 23 If they do not represent any fire insurance company in any 24 capacity.

Dues. 25 If they pay annual dues of ten dollars to the corporation.

MEMBERSHIP—CLASS FIVE.

Class Five. 26 The following described natural persons or firms may be 27 admitted to membership in Class Five upon the recommenda- 28 tion of two officials of the corporation: 29 If elected by the Executive Committee.

Business. 30 If they are principally engaged in the business of insurance.

Office. 31 If their residence and place of business is located outside of 32 Cook County, Illinois. 33 If they are in good standing in the place where their office 34 is located.

Dues. 35 If they pay annual dues of ten dollars to the corporation.

36 Members of any class, who shall for three months continu- 37 ously cease to have the qualifications necessary to membership

Ineligibles. 38 therein, shall cease to be members thereof, but may be admitted 39 to such other class as they may make application for, and be 40 qualified for admission to.

Partners. 41 New partners may be admitted into a firm holding a mem- 42 bership, if qualified for admission to membership in the class 43 held by the firm, and if approved by the vote required to admit 44 an applicant to a personal membership therein.

MEMBERSHIP AGREEMENT.

Membership Agreement.
Members are to agree to abide by, observe, and uphold the constitution, by-laws, rules, regulations, tariffs and rates, of the corporation, as now or hereafter made, and to enforce compliance therewith by all agents or others under his or their jurisdiction or control.

ARTICLE VII.

POWER TO VOTE.

Power to Vote.
Any person or firm, holding a membership in the corporation either as an officer of a fire insurance company, or, if there be no such officer holding such membership, as the Manager or General Agent of a fire insurance company, having, as such, superior and exclusive authority over the entire County of Cook, or, if there be no such officer or general agent, holding such membership as the sole and exclusive agent for a fire insurance company for the principal city district, is hereby qualified to vote, either in person or by proxy. No more than one vote shall be cast by any one member, or be based on the representation of any one company. Provided, that nothing contained in this section shall deprive any person or firm or any present member of a firm now (January 11th, 1906) holding a membership, of the power to vote, so long as they remain qualified for, and in continuous membership in, the class to which the persons or firms above described would be qualified for admission.

Proxy.
Members, qualified to vote, may delegate authority, in writing, to some one in their employ, to vote in their name, but not to another member.

ARTICLE VIII.

MEETINGS.

Meetings—Annual, Quarterly
Meetings of members shall be held quarterly on the second Thursday of January (which shall also be the annual meeting), April, July and October in each year, at such hour and place as may be provided by the Executive Committee. Notice of such meeting shall be sent to all members qualified to vote, at least three days prior thereto.

Special.
Special meetings may be called by a majority vote of the Executive Committee upon like notice or shall be called by the Executive Committee upon the written request of fifteen members qualified to vote. The notice of such special meetings shall clearly state the object thereof, and action taken be limited thereto.

ARTICLE IX.

QUORUM.

Quorum.
A quorum for the transaction of business shall consist of thirty-three members qualified to vote.

ARTICLE X.

ELECTIONS.

Elections— President. Vice President. Treasurer.	All elections shall be by ballot. The candidate receiving a majority of the votes cast shall be declared elected. Elections to the offices of President, Vice President and Treasurer shall be at the annual meetings of the corporation.
Executive Committee. Patrol Committee.	Elections to membership on the Executive Committee and Patrol Committee shall be as provided in Section 12 of this Constitution.
Manager. Secretary. Supt. of Ratings. Chief Surveyor.	Elections to the offices of Manager, Secretary, Superintendents of Ratings and Chief Surveyor shall be at the annual meeting held in 1906.
Vacancies.	Elections to fill vacancies shall be held at the next regular meeting after such vacancy shall occur. Where the vacancy existing is in an office having a definite term the election shall be for the unexpired term thereof, otherwise the election shall be for an indefinite term.
Nominations.	Nominations to the office of Manager may be made by the Executive Committee and to the offices of Secretary, Superintendents of Ratings and Chief Surveyor by the Manager, but this shall not prevent other nominations to such offices from being made at the meeting at which the election is held.

ARTICLE XI.

OFFICERS.

Officers.	The officers of the corporation shall consist of a President, a Vice President, a Treasurer, a Manager, a Secretary, two Superintendents of Ratings, and a Chief Surveyor.
Term.	The term of the office of the President, Vice President and Treasurer shall be one year, and until their successors shall have been elected and have been installed in office. The term of office of the Manager, Secretary, Superintendents of Ratings and Chief Surveyor shall be indefinite, but each and every of the persons elected thereto shall be subject to removal by the corporation on the recommendation of the Executive Committee.
Deputies.	Assistants or deputies to the Manager, the Secretary, the Superintendents of Ratings or the Chief Surveyor, may be appointed by the Manager with the advice and consent of the Executive Committee.

ARTICLE XII.

COMMITTEES.

Committees—	
Executive.	Executive: There shall be elected by ballot from the members an Executive Committee of twelve, not more than one being from any one firm, one-fourth of whom shall retire every three months; the retiring member and every member of his firm shall be ineligible for re-election for twelve months thereafter. Fifteen days before each quarterly meeting the President shall

appoint three members a committee who shall nominate a ticket with three names for membership on the Executive Committee. This special committee shall report through the Record ten days before the quarterly meeting. Five days before the quarterly meeting the Secretary shall publish in the Record any nomination for the Executive Committee that shall have received the written approval of the nominee endorsed by ten members holding authority to vote. These requirements shall not, however, prevent nominations of other persons for such positions at the quarterly meeting. At the annual meeting in January, 1906,

Term. there shall be elected three members to serve three months, three to serve six months, three to serve nine months, and three to serve one year, and thereafter there shall be elected at each quarterly meeting three members to serve one year.

President. The President shall be ex-officio, a member of the Executive Committee with power to vote, and the Vice President shall be,

Vice President. ex-officio, member of the committee, but shall not be entitled to vote, except in the absence of the President, unless also elected a member of the committee, to which membership he shall be eligible.

Chairman. The Manager shall be ex-officio, chairman of the committee without the power to vote.

Patrol. Patrol: At the annual meetings there shall be elected from the members two members of a Patrol Committee of six to serve for three years, not more than one member of the committee shall be from any one firm, provided that at the annual meeting in 1906 six members shall be elected, two for one, two for two and two for three years.

The committee charged with nominating members for membership on the Executive Committee to be voted upon at the annual meeting, shall also nominate a ticket with two names for members of a Patrol Committee, and other persons may be nominated for such positions at the annual meeting. The Patrol Committee, so chosen, may elect a seventh member, for a term of one year, from members of the corporation or from other contributors to the support of the Patrol.

Arbitration, Appeal— Fines, Penalties. Arbitration and Appeal—Fines and Penalties: The President may, from time to time, with the advice and consent of the Executive Committee, appoint a committee of not less than three in number, as may be deemed advisable, to act as a committee on arbitration and appeal, and in like manner, appoint a committee on fines and penalties. Appointments to such committees need not be confined to members of the corporation.

Classifications. Classifications: The salaried officers of the corporation shall constitute a committee on classifications, rates and schedules.

Special. Special: Special committees may be raised by resolution of the corporation or Executive Committee, and any committee may refer a subject to a sub-committee of its own members, but no such special committee or sub-committee shall have power to act

finally without the subsequent approval of the corporation or the larger committee respectively.

Vacancies. Vacancies in committees or sub-committees, when not otherwise provided for, may be filled for the unexpired time in the same manner as the original election or appointment was made.

ARTICLE XIII.

PATROLMEN'S PENSION FUND.

Patrolmen's Pension Fund. There shall be maintained a Patrolmen's Pension Fund as provided for by statute of the State of Illinois, which shall be administered as provided therein, and it shall be the duty of the President, Secretary, Treasurer and Chairman of the Patrol Committee to qualify for and serve upon "The Board of Trustees of the Patrolmen's Pension Fund" as provided by law.

Trustees.

ARTICLE XIV.

REVENUE.

Revenue. To provide for the expenses of the corporation, except the support and maintenance of the fire patrol, there shall be returned during the months of January and July of each year, by or on behalf of every company represented by a member, a

Returns. statement of the net premiums (deducting reinsurance premiums paid to members only) received by or for such company during the preceding six months, for insurance effected covering property situate in the County of Cook, State of Illinois. Returns

May be Consolidated. may be made by the several representatives, or may be consolidated and returned by the company or one of its representatives.

Assessment. The aggregate of such returns shall be the basis of assessment for the ordinary expenses of the corporation for the current half year, and the rate per cent. of the assessment shall be fixed by the Executive Committee. A separate account of dues,

Dues, Fees, Fines. fees and fines received by the corporation shall be kept, and such funds shall be expended only with the approval of a majority of the members of the corporation qualified to vote. The total

Publication. amount returned for each company, corporation, association, underwriter, agent or person contributing may be published.

Fire Patrol. To provide for the support and maintenance of a fire patrol, all insurance companies, corporations, associations, underwriters, agents or persons shall be required to make such returns, and pay such assessment as is provided by law. The funds received

Separate Funds. from such assessment shall be kept separate and apart from other funds of the corporation, and shall only be expended for the purposes described.

Publication. The total amount returned for each company, corporation, association, underwriter, agent or person contributing may be published.

ARTICLE XV.

WITHDRAWALS.

Withdrawals. Any member of Class Number One may withdraw from the corporation on giving thirty days written notice to the President of the corporation of his intention to do so; which shall be im-
Notice. mediately communicated to the Executive Committee. Unless such notice be recalled within ten days, it shall be communicated to the members of Class Number One and any other member thereof may withdraw at the same time, provided he has given at least five days' written notice to the President of the
Publication. corporation. All such notices shall be immediately communi-
Disregard of Obligations. cated to the members. A notice of intent to disregard any rule or obligation shall be construed as a notice of withdrawal.

Any member of any other class may withdraw without notice, but the fact shall be published to members.

Property of Board. Members withdrawing shall deliver to the corporation all books, cards or other records, showing the rates fixed by the corporation, and all of its furniture or other property in their possession. They shall also pay all assessments or dues up to the period of withdrawal.

ARTICLE XVI.

BY-LAWS—RULES.

By-Laws. The by-laws may prescribe the powers and duties of the several committees, officers, and agents of the corporation, the basis and methods of fixing rates, and the promulgation thereof, the method of procedure in investigating alleged breaches of the by-laws, rules, regulations, tariffs and rates, and provide penalties, therefor, and may prescribe such rules of practice as may be needful, and are not elsewhere provided, but no by-law may be adopted not in conformity with the charter and this constitution.

Rules for the government of members in matters not provided for in the constitution and by-laws, may be made at any meeting, by a majority vote of the qualified voters present.

ARTICLE XVII.

AMENDMENTS.

Amendments. The constitution may be altered or amended, at any regular meeting of the corporation, by an affirmative vote of three-fifths of the members qualified to vote, such of them, as are not present, being allowed to record their vote, in writing, within ten
Voting in Writing. days after the meeting. Provided, that previous notice of the proposed alteration or amendment has been mailed to all members at least ten days prior to the meeting.

BY-LAWS

President's Duties. SECTION 1. The President shall preside at all meetings of the corporation, and shall sign, as such officer, all checks and papers executed by or on behalf of the corporation as shall require the signature of such officer. He shall receive and lay before the members of the corporation at their meetings the report of the Executive and Patrol Committees and officers of the corporation, and generally do and perform such duties, pertaining to his office, as are not otherwise specially provided to be performed by some other officer or officers.

Vice President. SEC. 2. The Vice President, during the absence or disability of the President, or in case of his neglect or refusal to perform such duties, shall perform the duties and be vested with the powers of the President.

Treasurer. SEC. 3. The Treasurer shall receive from the Secretary or other person or persons the funds of the corporation and have charge thereof. He shall by, and with the advice and consent **Bank.** of the Executive Committee, select a bank or banks in which shall be deposited such funds. He shall sign all checks and see that proper vouchers are taken for all disbursements. **Bond.** He shall give such bond as the Executive Committee may require.

Manager. SEC. 4. The Manager shall have general direction and supervision of the affairs of the corporation and of the work of the Secretary, Superintendents of Ratings, Chief Surveyor and all employes, and shall have authority to require from them a proper performance of their duties, and shall be responsible to the Executive Committee for the same.

Duties. He shall perform such duties not otherwise provided for, as the corporation or Executive Committee may direct.

Power. He shall nominate candidates for Secretary, Superintendents of Ratings and Chief Surveyor as hereinbefore provided.

He shall have authority to employ, to suspend, or to discharge any employe of the corporation, subject to the approval of the Executive Committee.

He shall have the privilege of the floor at all meetings of the corporation and be chairman of the Executive Committee.

He shall be subject to removal at any time by the corporation on the recommendation of the Executive Committee.

Secretary. SEC. 5. The Secretary, under the direction and supervision of the Manager, shall perform the usual duties pertaining to his office, attend all meetings of the corporation and of the standing committees, and keep full minutes of the proceedings and action taken thereat. He shall collect from members assessments required by the constitution for the maintenance of the corporation, and all other moneys due the corporation, giving proper receipts therefor, paying such moneys to the Treasurer and taking his receipt for such payment. He shall keep correct books

of account. He shall draw all orders on the Treasurer for moneys disbursed, which orders must also be signed by the Manager, and take proper vouchers for such disbursements. He shall give such bonds as the Executive Committee may direct, and shall perform such other duties as the corporation or the Manager may direct. He shall be subject to removal at any time by the corporation on the recommendation of the Executive Committee.

Superintendents of Ratings.

Sec. 6. The Superintendents of Ratings, subject to the direction and supervision of the Manager, shall have charge of the ratings of all risks within the jurisdiction of the corporation. In accordance with the provisions of the by-laws they shall apply accurately all schedules and tariffs adopted by the corporation for making rates. They shall keep a correct copy of all rates so made. They shall promulgate same to members only, in such manner as the by-laws, the corporation or the Manager may prescribe, and perform such other duties as the corporation or Manager may direct.

They shall be subject to removal at any time by the corporation on the recommendation of the Executive Committee.

Chief Surveyor.

Sec. 7. The Chief Surveyor, subject to the direction and supervision of the Manager, shall have charge of the making of such surveys and inspections as may be required for the complete knowledge of the property within the jurisdiction of the corporation, necessary to form an intelligent judgment as to the condition of the risks. He shall keep accurate records of all such inspections, and publish fully and impartially to members only such information and in such manner as the corporation or the Manager may prescribe, and perform such other duties as the corporation or the Manager may direct. He shall be subject to removal at any time by the corporation on the recommendation of the Executive Committee.

POWERS AND DUTIES OF COMMITTEES.

EXECUTIVE.

Executive Committee— Power and Duties.

Sec. 8. Regular meetings of the committee shall be held at such times and places as it may designate. Special meetings may be held when called by the President, by the Chairman or by three members of the committee in writing, at least 24 hours' notice shall be given of all special meetings.

Affairs of Corporation.

The committee shall have the management of all of the affairs of the corporation, unless otherwise provided for, and may, with the concurrence of two-thirds of its membership, establish rules for its own conduct that shall not conflict herewith, which rules may only be changed by a like concurrence, after one week's notice to members qualified to vote.

Construe Constitution, etc.

It may construe the provisions of the constitution, by-laws and rules, such construction to be literal, where possible, and to be subject to appeal, by any three members of the corporation,

Expenditures. qualified to vote, in writing, to the next meeting of the corporation. It shall supervise and control all current expenditures of the corporation, except those made in behalf of the fire patrol. It shall approve no expenditure of money in excess of one hundred dollars at any one time for other than current expenses, such as rent, light, heat, office supplies, postage, printing, salaries, wages rewards, traveling and legal expenses.

Revenue. It shall fix the rate per cent. to be assessed on premiums reported by members, for the expenses of the current half year.

It shall cause to be kept full and complete minutes of its meetings, and have information of any action of a general character, taken by it, published to members qualified to vote.

Record. It may authorize the publication of an inquiry sheet—to be called the Record—from time to time, which shall be sent to such class or classes of members as answers may be required from.

Report. It shall make an annual report to the membership, covering the business of the preceding year, and such special reports and recommendations, from time to time, as may be agreed upon.

Auditor. It shall have the receipts and disbursements of the corporation audited by independent accountants at least once each year.

Bureau on Affairs outside County. A bureau under the direction of a Manager with such other officers and representatives as may be necessary in the conduct of the affairs of the corporation outside of the County of Cook may be created by concurrence of the Executive Committee.

PATROL.

Patrol—Powers and Duties. The Patrol Committee shall have control over the patrol, and supervise the expenditure of the funds raised for its maintenance and support, which shall be kept separate and apart from other funds of the corporation, and be disbursed, in payment of the expenses of the patrol, on vouchers approved by a majority of the patrol committee.

ARBITRATION AND APPEAL.

Arbitration and Appeal—Powers and Duties. The Committee on Arbitration and Appeal shall have the power, by the concurrence of a majority thereof, to render final judgment in any controversy between members, that may be voluntarily submitted to its decision by the members parties to the controversy.

FINES AND PENALTIES.

Fines and Penalties—Powers and Duties. The Committee on Fines and Penalties shall have the power to inflict fines upon any of the members of the corporation for breach of its by-laws, rules, regulations, tariffs and rates, to pass upon the question as to whether such breach has been committed or not, and whether it is wilful or has been done through error.

The method of investigating alleged breaches, and the fines

that may be imposed therefor shall be as provided in the by-laws.

CLASSIFICATIONS.

Classification. The Committee on Classifications may, where the schedule or tariff does not provide recognition thereof, make allowances for the superior construction of buildings, shall supervise all average rates and rates not fixed by schedule, may, with the concurrence of the Executive Committee, establish new or change old classifications under any schedule, when the Executive Committee by an affirmative vote of three-fourths of its whole number so directs, it may fix other than schedule rates on a preferred or sprinklered risk, and promulgate the same together with the manner in which the risk may be placed, and the brokerage (if any) allowable thereon.

Revision of Schedules. It shall, from time to time, revise old schedules and propose new ones, as may be necessary, or as may be required by the corporation or the Executive Committee, but such revisions and new schedules shall be subject to approval by vote of members so qualified.

Rates. SEC. 9. Rates. Schedules may be adopted for rating the several classes of risks, and specific rates shall be made in accordance therewith. Where an existing schedule does not apply, **Specific Average.** the specific rate made shall require the concurrence of the Classification Committee. Average rates based on a written statement of values by the owner may be made on all property, except grain elevators and contents, storage warehouses and contents, property situate in the Union Stock Yards district, and property used for the manufacture and or storage of packing house products in Cook County, Illinois. Statements of values and average rates shall be revised annually and shall require the concurrence of the Classification Committee. Specific rates shall be made by the Superintendents of Ratings and be by them **Publication.** promulgated to members. Those relating to property in the principal city district simultaneously to members of Class Number One, and those relating to other property in the County of Cook simultaneously to members of Class Number One, and such members of Class Number Two as may request them.

Advance Information. Provided, that advance information may be given to members, writing or placing the entire insurance on the property on which the rating or re-rating is contemplated, upon application from such member who shall first file a written statement that he does in fact at that time control the entire insurance so involved; and provided, further, that, when a reduction in rate has **Reduction.** been denied a member, no reduction shall thereafter be considered in such rate without twenty-four hours' previous notice to such member, record of such refusals to be made by private mark on the survey.

Private Mark. Provided, however, that no private mark of any member shall be put upon any survey until such member as aforesaid shall first file a written statement with the Superintendent of Ratings that he controls the whole or part of the risk affected.

Mis-statements or mis-representations in an application for advance information as to rates shall be treated the same as violations of other rules.

Existing Rates Binding.

The promulgated rate, as it appears in the minimum tariff and on the printed books, rate cards and sheets, is the existing minimum rate of the corporation and is binding on members from the date of publication shown thereon, and no policy shall be written at a rate less than that existing at the time the risk is accepted.

Mutual Plan of Policy.

The money consideration paid for the policy shall be a fixed sum stated therein, and shall not be subject to increase by assessment or otherwise, except for increase in hazard or for additional privileges granted thereunder, nor shall such fixed sum be decreased by rebate, participation in profits or otherwise, except for promulgated reduction in rate with authority to rebate therefor stated with the publication of the rate. No rebate shall be made on a cancelled or expired policy. If the rebate authorized is subject to a stipulation to be endorsed on the policy, no rebate shall be allowed without endorsing such stipulation on the policy.

Rebate.

Application for Specific Rates.

When there is no existing specific rate, and the minimum tariff is not applicable to the risk, and whenever there has been a change in the ownership, construction, occupancy or occupants of the risk or of the schedule applicable thereto, since the publication of the existing rate, insurance covering the risk in whole or in part shall not be written until the rates thereon have been made or revised and published, provided, that binders subject to the payment of the new rate may be issued for a period of not more than 30 days.

Binders.

Minimum.

Insurance on property south of Harrison street and north and west of the Chicago river may be written under the Minimum Tariff if occupied or to be occupied for the following purposes only:

(a) Charitable Institutions
(b) Churches
(c) Club Houses
(d) Dwellings
(e) Flats
(f) Halls without scenery
(g) Offices
(h) Private Boarding Houses
(i) Private Stables
(j) Public Institutions
(k) Schools

Fire Maps.

In applying the Minimum Tariff the fire maps shall be taken as the guide in ascertaining exposures and distances between risks, and, whenever any question arises relative to the application of the Minimum Tariff, the subject shall be referred to the Superintendents of Ratings, who may make a discretionary rate and promulgate the same.

Reduction in Meeting.

No reduction of specific rates shall be made at a meeting of

1 the corporation without the affirmative vote of a majority of all
2 of its members qualified to vote, nor unless twenty-four hours prior
3 written notice of the proposed reduction has been given such
4 members by the Secretary, and the fact that such reductions are
5 to be proposed is stated in the call or notice for the meeting.

Vote.
6 The vote of members on the question of reduction of specific
7 rates shall be by ballot, and members qualified to vote not pres-
8 ent at the meeting, shall have the privilege of voting on the
9 question through The Record within five days after the date of
10 the meeting.

Short Rates.
11 All insurance written for a term less than one year shall be
12 charged for at the established short rates, except when written
13 in lieu of insurance cancelled, in accordance with the rule gov-
14 erning cancellations.

Promulgated Rate Binding.
15 The customary rates now being charged by members, as
16 shown by the published records in their possession are binding
17 on them until others are established and promulgated as pro-
18 vided in this by-law.

Contribution.
19 SEC. 10. Contribution. The rates and forms adopted by
20 this corporation shall be predicated on there being insurance
21 equal to at least eighty per cent of the value at risk, and all poli-
22 cies written by members shall contain an eighty per cent contri-
23 bution clause as part of the consideration for the policy, pro-
24 vided, that other percentages of value may be agreed upon as
25 hereinafter provided, to wit:

Agreed Percentages.
26 Agreed percentages shall be fixed at either 50, 60, 70, 80, 90
27 or 100 per cent. of the value at risk, where the subject of insur-
28 ance is not required to be insured under a prescribed form re-
29 quiring some other percentage.

Fifty Per Cent.
30 Where 50 per cent. is agreed upon, 40 per cent. must be add-
31 ed to the published rate.

Sixty.
32 Where 60 per cent. is agreed upon, 20 per cent. must be
33 added to the published rate.

Seventy.
34 Where 70 per cent. is agreed upon, 10 per cent must be
35 added to the published rate.

Ninety.
36 Where 90 per cent. is agreed upon and the only subject of
37 insurance is building, 5 per cent. may be deducted from the pub-
38 lished rate.

One Hundred Per Cent.
39 Where 100 per cent. is agreed upon and the only subject of
40 insurance is building, 10 per cent. may be deducted from the pub-
41 lished rate.

Blanket.
42 Provided, that when buildings are incorporated with other
43 subjects in general or blanket forms, with 90%, or full contribu-
44 tion, the same allowance may be made on building rate in com-
45 puting average rates, as would be allowed where they are specific-
46 ally or separately insured.

Insurance Without Co-insurance.
47 Insurance covering the following described risks may be
48 written without any co-insurance, viz.:
49   (a) Dwellings and contents
50   (b) Flats and contents

(c) Household furniture, except when contained in a public storage warehouse.

(d) Liability of railroad and transportation companies as common carriers, the advance charges of same

(e) Private stables and contents

(f) Vessels laid up

(g) One-story buildings, stores only, or stores and dwellings and their contents, except stocks, south of Harrison Street and north and west of the Chicago River

(h) Stores and flats and their contents, except stocks, south of Harrison Street and north and west of the Chicago River

Flats and Apartment Buildings. "Provided, that all flats and apartment buildings covering more than fifty feet of frontage and being over three stories in height shall be specifically rated before being written and that the publication of the rate shall carry with it the use of the 80 per cent. contribution clause."

COMMISSIONS—BROKERAGES.

Commissions. SEC. 11. For the purpose of grading the commissions to be paid or received, property is hereby divided into two classes, to be designated and known as Ordinary and Preferred. The Ordinary class shall comprise all property not hereinafter classed as preferred. The Preferred class shall consist of buildings occupied exclusively for either or all of the following purposes, south of Harrison Street and north and west of the Chicago River.

Ordinary

Preferred.

(a) Apartment Houses and contents
(b) Charitable Institutions and contents
(c) Churches and contents
(d) Club Houses and contents
(e) Dwellings and contents
(f) Flats and contents
(g) Halls without scenery and contents
(h) Offices and contents
(i) Private Boarding Houses and contents
(j) Private Stables and contents
(k) Public Institutions and contents
(l) School Houses and contents
(m) One-story Buildings, stores only or stores and dwellings
(n) Stores and flats
(o) Store and Apartment Houses
(p) Contents of buildings described in sections (m), (n), and (o) except stocks of merchandise, and fixtures for same, occupying 5,000 sq. ft. or more of ground area.

Brokerage— Class One. Members of Class Number One, on interchange of business with each other, may pay and receive brokerages thereon as follows: On ordinary business, 10 per cent., and on preferred business, 25 per cent. of the premium.

Class Two.

1 Members of Class Number One, on interchange of business
2 with members of Class Number Two, may pay and receive
3 brokerage thereon as follows: If the property be located outside
4 of the principal city district, on ordinary business, 10 per cent.,
5 and on preferred business, 25 per cent. If the property be loca-
6 ted within the principal city district, on buildings, leaseholds and
7 rents of the ordinary class, 10 per cent., and on all preferred
8 business, 25 per cent.

9 Members of Class Number Two, on interchange of business
10 with each other, may pay and receive brokerage thereon as
11 follows: On ordinary business, 10 per cent., and on preferred
12 business, 25 per cent. of the premium, and on policies actually
13 issued by them as agents may charge and receive on ordinary
14 business, 15 per cent., and on preferred business, 25 per cent.

Class Three.

15 Members of Class Number Three, on business placed with
16 members who are policy writing representatives of companies,
17 may be paid brokerages as follows: On ordinary business, 10
18 per cent., and on preferred business, 25 per cent.

Class Four.

19 Members of Class Number Four, on business placed with
20 members who are policy writing representatives of companies,
21 may be paid brokerages as follows: On buildings, leaseholds
22 and rents, if ordinary business, 10 per cent.; if preferred business,
23 25 per cent.

Class Five.

24 Members of Class Number Five, on business placed with
25 members who are policy writing representatives of companies,
26 may be paid brokerages as follows: On all classes of property,
27 10 per cent.

28 No commission, brokerage or consideration of any kind shall
29 be allowed to other than a member in good standing, except by
30 a member to his own registered solicitor, as provided, and no
31 other or greater allowance than the commission herein provided
32 for in the way of brokerage, gifts, gratuities or otherwise, shall
33 be permissible between members. The offering, promising, ma-
34 king, asking or taking of any other or greater allowance by a
35 member is hereby expressly forbidden.

Date from which Commission may be paid.

36 The right to receive brokerage on interchange of business
37 between members shall exist from the date of their application
38 for membership, or if suspended, from date of reinstatement in
39 good standing.

SOLICITORS.

Solicitors.

40 SEC. 12. The privileges extended by this corporation are per-
41 sonal. Members may, however, take into their exclusive employ per-
42 sons to solicit and place business with or through them in such
43 numbers as they may see fit, and compensate them by salary or
44 commission as may be agreed upon between them, providing such

Eligibility.

45 solicitors be exclusively engaged in the same business as the
46 employer, give their whole time to his service, have their sole
47 office with him, place their entire business with or through him,
48 and be registered with the corporation as qualified to be, and as,
49 employed by a member.

Responsibility.

50 Members are responsible for the acts of their solicitors, and

Commission.

other employes, in the same manner and to the same extent as though the act was their own, and the qualifications of persons presented for registration are subject to the supervision of the corporation.

When a solicitor or registered office employe is compensated by commission it may be at the same rate as the employer would be entitled to receive on business placed by him with another member.

Term.

The registration of a solicitor or office employe shall fix his status for one year from date thereof, during which time dealings with him shall be exclusively upon and for account of the employer, and change in employment from one member to another shall require the written consent of the member in whose employ the person is registered for the time being.

Fees.

Registration fees may be required as follows: For persons employed daily *in* the office of a member at least seven hours, and for the first six solicitors, not so employed, one dollar each per annum, and for each additional not so employed, one hundred dollars per annum.

DEALINGS WITH NON-MEMBERS—SUSPENDED MEMBERS.

Non-members.

SEC. 13. Whenever a member is unable to procure the insurance required from members of the corporation on regular terms, he may then, but not until then, place such with or through persons or companies not members of or represented by members of the corporation, under the form prescribed and at the rate fixed by the corporation. He shall report such fact to the Secretary within

Surp'us Insurance.

the twenty-four hours next ensuing, and the same shall be published to members of Class Number One. If it shall subsequently appear that the insurance could have been had on regular terms from members the member shall be chargeable with a violation of this rule.

Commission to.

Members may receive from and write or place insurance for not-affiliated persons or companies, or for suspended members, under the form prescribed and at the rate fixed by the corporation, but shall not allow any brokerage, commission, discount drawback, rebate, or consideration in any form, either directly or indirectly, therefor.

Delinquents.

SEC. 14. Delinquents. When any member shall be delinquent in the payment of premiums for more than sixty days after the close of the month in which the policy was issued, a notice of such delinquency may be sent to the Secretary, who may notify the members of Classes One and Two that the delinquent member is suspended during his delinquency, and no commission shall be allowed or paid to the delinquent until he shall have been reinstated in good standing and notice given thereof.

DISCIPLINE.

Discipline.

SEC. 15. Alleged breaches of the by-laws, rules, regulations, tariffs and rates shall be investigated by an officer or agent of the

Investigation.

corporation. If, from such investigation, it shall appear that a

Error.	breach has been committed, that it was committed through error, but that no member has suffered loss of business, theretofore had by him, thereby, he may require correction of the error. If the member guilty of such breach does not correct the error within three business days, and, or, if it shall appear that a mem-
Wilful.	ber has lost business, theretofore had by him, through such error, or in case it shall appear that a wilful breach has been com- mitted, the officer or agent shall report such finding to the Com- mittee on Fines and Penalties, who shall cite the accused to appear before it, at a time fixed within the next five business days, and show cause why such finding should not be confirmed.
Trial.	If the accused does not appear, at the time fixed, or does not establish the fact that he is innocent of the breach alleged, to the satisfaction of the committee, the finding of the officer or agent shall be confirmed, and the committee shall fix a fine or penalty therefor, which for breach through error shall not be
Fine.	less than five dollars, nor more than fifty dollars, in the discre- tion of the committee, for wilful breach, the fine shall be fixed at not less than twenty-five dollars nor more than two hundred and fifty dollars, in the discretion of the committee, and, unless the convicted member perfects an appeal as hereinafter provided, he shall stand suspended until the fine or penalty has been sat- isfied.
Appeal.	The convicted member may appeal from the finding of the Committee on Fines and Penalties to the Executive Committee in the manner following: He shall within twenty-four hours after being notified of the result of the hearing before the Com- mittee on Fines and Penalties, file a notice of such appeal with the Executive Committee, and at the same time deposit with the
Deposit.	Secretary of the corporation a sum of money equal in amount to twice the fine or penalty fixed by the Committee on Fines and Penalties. The perfection of an appeal, as above provided, shall continue the member in the privileges of membership, pending the hearing thereof by the Executive Committee, before whom the convicted member shall prosecute such appeal to a conclusion within the next fifteen business days after notice thereof has been filed with the Executive Committee.
Decision. Fine.	The appeal shall be heard by such members of the Executive Committee (not less than a majority in number) as are not interested in the case as accuser or accused. If the convicted member does not appear at the time fixed by the committee to hear the appeal, or does not prosecute the appeal to a conclusion as aforesaid, or does not within said fifteen days establish his innocence of the breach alleged, to the satisfaction of two-thirds of the members of the Executive Committee sitting in the hear- ing of the appeal, the finding of the Committee on Fines and Penalties shall be affirmed, the Executive Committee may revise the amount of the fine or penalty fixed, and may fix the same at not less than one-half of, nor more than twice, the amount of that fixed by the Committee on Fines and Penalties, and unless the convicted member perfects an appeal to the Board as here-

inafter provided, the difference between the fine or penalty imposed and the deposit made (if any) shall be returned to the member after the expiration of the time in which he could appeal.

Appeal to Board. The convicted member may appeal from the finding of the Executive Committee to a meeting of the members qualified to vote, by filing a notice of such appeal with the President or Secretary, within twenty-four hours after he has been notified of the decision of the Executive Committee, and at the same time depositing with the Secretary of the corporation such additional sum of money as may be necessary to make his deposit equal to twice the amount of the fine or penalty confirmed or fixed by the Executive Committee, but the deposit shall not be less than that originally made. The perfection of an appeal as above provided, shall continue him in the privileges of membership, pending the hearing thereof by a meeting of members qualified to vote. The appeal shall be heard by such members, qualified to vote (not less than a quorum in number), as are not interested in the case as accuser or accused, at a special meeting to be called for that purpose, and held within one week from date of filing the notice of appeal.

Decision.
Fine. If the convicted member does not, at such special meeting or at an adjourned session thereof, establish his innocence of the breach alleged, to the satisfaction of three-fifths of the disinterested members present and qualified to vote as aforesaid, the previous findings shall be the final judgment of the Board, which may revise the fine or penalty imposed and fix the same at not less than that confirmed or fixed by the Executive Committee, nor more than the sum deposited with the corporation by the accused, and there may be passed a vote censuring or temporarily suspending the privilege of membership, or, by a three-fifths vote of all members qualified to vote, expelling him from membership.

Procedure. The method of procedure by or before the Committee on Fines and Penalties, the Executive Committee and or, the Board shall be as prescribed by the Executive Committee. Provided,
Vote. that the votes taken at such meetings shall be by ballot, and that neither the accused or other person shall be represented by professional counsel.

Reward. The Executive Committee is authorized to offer a reward of not more than one thousand dollars to any person who shall furnish evidence that does finally convict any member guilty of a breach of the rules regulating the payment of commission, or guilty of rebating to the assured.

Record. SEC. 16. The Secretary, under the supervision of the Executive Committee, shall publish, as often as may be necessary, a private bulletin—called The Record—which shall be sent to such class or classes of members as are desired to respond thereto.

Signatures thereto shall be by the number assigned the member, to which each member shall be furnished the key. Clear, direct and explicit answers to all queries made through The

Record are obligatory on all members to which it is sent, and must be made within forty-eight hours after receipt of The Record.

Failure to answer, or answering untruthfully, are offenses punishable the same as other offenses.

Amendments. SEC. 17. These by-laws may be altered or amended at any regular meeting of the corporation by three-fifths of all the constitutional votes, members not present being allowed to vote through The Record at any time within one week after the meeting, provided, that one week's notice of such proposed alteration or amendment has been given to all voting members.

RULES

ACETYLENE GAS.

Permission may be granted for the generation and use of Acetylene Gas under the form as noted below, but not otherwise: For form of permit for the use of Acetylene Gas see page 60

NOTE.—See Calcium Carbide, page 33.

ADDITIONAL PREMIUMS.

In all cases where a permit is endorsed on an existing policy granting a privilege not charged for in the original premium charged, for which a charge is required to be made under the rules, and in all cases where notice is published of an advance in rate, for increase in hazard arising from bad condition of the premises, or for withdrawal of protection from the premises, and the notice requires additional premium to be collected on existing insurance, additional premium pro rata of the advance in rate for the unexpired time of the policy shall be charged and collected.

ADJUSTMENT CLAUSE.

The use of an adjustment clause which in any way does away with the conditions of the policies is prohibited.

ASSIGNMENTS.

(See also page 38.)

No consent shall be given to the assignment of any policy or certificate covering in any elevator or storage warehouse, and such policies or certificates, if cancelled, must be cancelled at usual short rates.

NOTE.—Assignments must be made on the policy or certificate. See Endorsements.

AUTOMOBILES.

Privilege to keep automobiles or similar vehicles using gasoline, naphtha, or other volatile hydro-carbon oils for fuel, or power, may be granted under form as noted below and in consideration of additional annual premium but not otherwise.

For form of permits for Automobiles using Gasoline, see page 63.

AVERAGE CLAUSE.

Where policies are written on two or more buildings separated by a brick wall without openings, or with openings pro-

tected with approved fire doors, or by open space, or on iron storage tanks not housed, or on the contents of such buildings or storage tanks, the average clause shall in all cases be used, unless written under the conditions governing blanket insurance. (See also pages 32 and 42.)

In all cases where policies are written covering on or in two or more buildings or places, having different rates, under the average clause, it shall be necessary for such risks to be rated by the Superintendent of Ratings and an average rate promulgated; otherwise the highest rate on any part of the property shall prevail.

For forms of Average Clause, see page 65.

NOTE.—Insurance cannot be written to cover the contents of more than one elevator or storage warehouse under the same item. (See "Elevator and Warehouse Insurance," page 37.)

BENZINE, GASOLINE, NAPHTHA, ETC.

(For forms for use of Benzine, etc., see pages 75, 76, 77, 96.)

Permission may be granted for the use, handling or storage of benzine, gasoline, mineral turpentine, naphtha and other light products of petroleum, and for the use of permitted devices using same for fuel, light or power, subject to the restrictions following, but not otherwise.

The quantity of either or all of the light products of petroleum permitted shall not exceed one gallon (exclusive of not exceeding one gallon contained in the device), to be kept in approved metal safety cans, for each occupant of a building, unless a rate be promulgated including a charge for the excess, or for a different method of storage, and the maximum quantity to be allowed be published with the rate, and no larger quantity shall be permitted than the maximum quantity stated.

No permit shall be granted for the use of any device using gasoline or other light product of petroleum for fuel, light or power (except it be the ordinary gasoline stove used for domestic purposes) unless the device of whatever nature is published on the Board's list of permitted devices, or a rate be promulgated including a charge for the use of the device, notice thereof to be published with the rate.

The classification committee is authorized to make special permits for the use of gasoline, benzine and other light products of petroleum, the tenor of such permits to be printed on the rate cards.

BINDERS.

Pending the issue of policies or certificates, binders good for not exceeding thirty days may be issued covering the risk in the interim, under form as noted below, but not otherwise.

For form for Binder, see page 117.

BLANKET INSURANCE.

Insurance covering under one sum separate or distinct risks or items of hazard separately rated, is blanket insurance.

Two or more separate subjects of insurance in specifically named location or locations, may be written under a blanket form of policy with the 90 per cent. co-insurance clause attached, at an average rate previously established and promulgated by the Superintendent of Ratings, but not otherwise. Provided, that if the insurance covers on or in two or more separate sections of the building, or on or in two or more separate buildings, or iron storage tanks not housed, the average clause shall also be attached unless the 100 per cent. co-insurance clause be attached in lieu of the 90 per cent. clause, in which case the average clause need not be used. NOTE: The 5 per cent. exception clause cannot be used. (See Contribution, page 23.)

(For Average Clauses, see page 65.)
(For Contribution Clause, see page 73.)

BREWERIES.

(See also page 42.)

Insurance covering breweries shall be written specifically as to the following items: $...... on building; $...... on machinery, fixtures, furniture and tools; $...... on stock.

BROKERAGE.

Members, registered solicitors and registered clerks are entitled to commissions on business placed by them at not exceeding the rates named by the Board from and after the date of their applications for membership or registration.

BUILDING INSURANCE.

When any mercantile or manufacturing business is carried on in any building of dwelling construction it shall be treated as a mercantile building under the Minimum Tariff, unless a specific rate is applied for and promulgated thereon, such specific rate to be subject to the discretion of the Superintendents of Ratings. (See also page 45.)

When any part of a building, improvements thereto or decorations thereof are separately insured for other than the owner of the building the insurance shall be written at the contents rate. (See also page 41.)

Insurance written to cover any unoccupied building having a published specific rate shall contain the following condition: "The premium charged herefor being for the hazard of the building unoccupied, it is understood and agreed that when occupied in whole or in part, notice shall be given this company at once

and payment made of additional premium, if any, required to cover the hazard of such occupancy, and the same condition shall be inserted in the policy when the rate is reduced for the same cause and a rebate made on the policy." (See also page 67.)

Foundations below the level of the under surface of the lowest basement floor may be excluded from being covered by the policy, but no other portion of the structure shall be so excluded.

Insurance written to cover buildings—unless the risk be a mill or manufactory—may also cover machinery pertaining to the service of the building or the furnishing of power therein, the property of the owner of the building, but no manufacturing machine or apparatus shall be included with the building. (See also page 41.)

NOTE.—Privileges of occupancy must be restricted. (See Occupancy, page 40.)

BUILDINGS IN PROCESS OF CONSTRUCTION.

Buildings in process of construction, south of Harrison Street and north and west of the Chicago River, to be occupied exclusively for

(a) Charitable Institutions.
(b) Churches.
(c) Club Houses.
(d) Dwellings.
(e) Flats.
(f) Halls without scenery.
(g) Offices.
(h) Private Boarding Houses.
(i) Private Stables.
(j) Public Institutions.
(k) Schools may be written under the Minimum Tariff and for a term of years with privilege to complete.

Permission for occupancy must always be stated in the policy and must be limited to the occupancies named above.

No other building in process of construction shall be written for a longer term than one year.

NOTE.—Occupancy privileges must be restricted. (See Occupancy, page 40.)

CALCIUM CARBIDE.

Not more than one hundred pounds of Calcium Carbide shall be permitted without additional charge, which additional charge must be fixed by the Superintendents of Ratings, and included in the published rate, prior to granting the permit.

Permits when granted without additional charge must be under form as noted below.

For form of Permit for Storage of Calcium Carbide, see page 67.)

Foundations below the level of the under surface of the lowest basement floor, or where there is no basement, below the surface of the ground, also the foundations of machinery below the surface of the ground, may be excluded from being covered by the policy, but no other portion of the structure shall be so excluded.

CANCELLATIONS.

Policies, certificates or binders may be cancelled pro rata:
(a) when done at the request of the company;
(b) where the entire amount of the policy, certificate or binder is immediately rewritten covering the same property for a term not less than the unexpired time;
(c) where the entire amount of the policy, certificate or binder is immediately rewritten covering the same property and the new premium charged is not less than the unearned premium on that cancelled;
(d) where the place of business or residence of the assured is removed to a new location, together with the entire subject insured, and the company is unable or unwilling to transfer its policy to cover in such new location.

Policies, certificates or binders MUST be cancelled at the established short rate:
(e) when done at the request of the assured;
(f) where the insurance to be cancelled covers the contents of an elevator or public storage warehouse;
(g) where the insurance is cancelled, to be rewritten at a lower rate without a promulgated improvement in risk;
(h) in all other cases not provided for under the provisions designated as "a," "b," "c," or "d."

CHANGE IN RISK.

When permission is granted under existing policies for any change in construction, hazard or occupancy, a new rate shall be applied for and additional premium, if any, collected.

No permit shall be granted for an opening to be made in a wall separating two buildings, or in a fire wall separating any two divisions of a building, without the prior approval of the Superintendents of Ratings and the payment of the additional premium, if any, required.

No permit shall be granted which will relieve the assured from his obligation to notify the company of any increase of hazard from such changes as may come to his knowledge.

No stipulation shall be inserted in any policy providing that it shall not be invalidated by the act of another committed without the knowledge or consent of the assured.

When a change in occupancy of a building takes the risk from the "ordinary" to the "preferred" class under term rates, although there may be no improvement in the risk, members are permitted to cancel policies pro rata and rewrite at "preferred" term rate.

COAL SHEDS.

(See also page 42.)

Insurance covering coal sheds may be so written as to include hoisting machinery therein.

COMMISSION AND PROFITS.

(See also page 41.)

No insurance covering merchandise shall be written so as to include commissions or profits thereon. Commissions and profits when insured shall be insured as a specific subject, at the rate of premium charged for the merchandise of or in the hands of the assured, and policies shall have the 80 per cent. co-insurance clause attached.

COMMON CARRIERS' LIABILITY.

(See also page 41.)

Insurance of the liability of common carriers when not included in a schedule of railroad property shall be restricted to their legal liability for baggage, wares and merchandise of others, in their possession as common carriers, and shall be upon forms provided by the Board or Executive Committee. The rate charged for such insurance shall not be less than that of the contents of the building containing the property.

CONSEQUENTAL DAMAGE.

Liability for consequential loss or damage must not be assumed under any policy insuring against direct loss or damage. The clause noted below shall be attached to all policies, except those insuring brewery property, covering on merchandise, stocks or products in houses artificially cooled other than solely by the storage of ice.

For form for Consequential Damage Clause, see page 70.

Where buildings containing the property insured have but one source supply for refrigerating purposes the form noted below shall be used in insuring against consequential damage, which must always be a specific policy and not by endorsement. The rate to be charged under this form shall be 50 per cent. of the rate on the equipment of the building or buildings containing the apparatus or equipment for refrigeration. *The assuming of this liability by endorsement prohibited. Specific policies covering only against consequential damage to be issued in all cases.*

Form Number One.

Single source equipment to be used where but one source supply for refrigeration is maintained. The charge under this form to be 50 per cent. of the rate on the equipment in the building containing refrigerating apparatus.

For Consequential Damage Form No. 1. see page 70.

When the rate cards state that buildings containing the property insured are provided with at least two sources of refrigeration, approved by the Superintendents of Ratings, each independent of the other and each of sufficient capacity to protect all the property in the houses connected therewith, and all kept in readiness for immediate use at all times, and so located that in the judgment of the Superintendents of Ratings they are not subject to one or the same fire, the form noted below shall be used. Insurance against consequential damage to be by specific policies only and not by endorsement. The rate where this form is used shall be 25 per cent. of the highest rated equipment furnishing refrigeration referred to herein.

(Two-source equipment.)

Form No. 2 to be used in covering against consequential damage where two sources of supply for refrigeration (not exposed to each other) are maintained, the two-source supply having had the approval of the Superintendents of Ratings. *The assuming of this insurance by endorsement prohibited. Specific policies to be issued.*

The premium charged to be 25 per cent. of the highest rated equipment furnishing refrigeration referred to herein.

For Consequential Damage Form No. 2, see page 71.

CONTENTS INSURANCE.

Insurance written to cover merchandise in any building shall not exclude any portion thereof.

Metals in ingots and pigs and scrap metal are excepted from the foregoing rule, and may be separately rated by the Superintendents of Ratings.

Insurance written to cover merchandise shall not be written for a term exceeding fifteen months. (See also pages 50 and 59.)

Insurance written to cover merchandise shall not include store furniture and fixtures under the same item unless written under the conditions governing blanket insurance. (See also page 42.)

Insurance written to cover merchandise contained in any public storage warehouse must exclude tobacco and its products unless the rate paid is that to be paid for insurance on tobacco. (See also page 42.)

Insurance written to cover furniture and fixtures must be written at the rate of the other contents belonging to the same assured, and if written for a term, under the same term rate rule as the building containing them. Electric light plants and other electrical apparatus may be insured as part of the furniture and fixtures, but policies covering electrical apparatus must contain the following clause: "This insurance does not cover any loss or damage to electrical machinery, apparatus and connections, caused by electric currents, whether artificial or natural."

CRUDE PETROLEUM.

Permission may be granted for the use of crude petroleum or fuel oil for fuel when the apparatus has been installed in accordance with the rules of the Board, but not otherwise. Permits when granted must be under form noted below.

For form for the use of Crude Petroleum or Fuel Oil, see page 73.

ELECTRIC LIGHT AND POWER GENERATING PLANTS RATED AS SUCH AND THOSE OPERATED IN CONNECTION WITH RAILWAYS.

(See also page 42.)

Policies covering electric light or power generating plants, either alone or with other property, must be written specifically as to the following sub-divisions:

Building (or building, boilers and engines), $......

Motors, switchboards, dynamos, wiring and connections, $......

Other contents of the building, $......

unless insured under the conditions governing blanket insurance.

All policies covering dynamos or other electric apparatus used for generating or distributing the electric current shall contain the following clause: "This Company shall not be liable for any loss or damage resulting from any electrical injury or disturbance, whether from artificial or natural cause, in or to any of the electrical apparatus, machinery, or connections hereby insured unless fire ensues, and then for loss resulting from fire only," and if lightning clause be attached to the policy it shall also except as to such loss.

ELEVATORS.

(See also page 42.)

Insurance covering grain or malt elevators or grain or malt warehouses may be written so as to include machinery, fixtures and millwright work, tools and implements therein.

Insurance shall not be written to cover the contents of more than one elevator or grain storage warehouse under the same item.

Insurance covering property contained in any elevator or grain storage warehouse may be transferred to cover the same property for the same owner in a new location where there is an actual removal of the property to such new location, but not otherwise; it shall not be assigned, and when cancelled it shall be at the usual short rates. It may contain a provision providing that the pledge of the property as collateral shall not make it

invalid, and may have attached a clause making the loss payable to another as follows: "Loss, if any, payable to ....or order hereon, but this insurance is void as to any subsequent owner or purchaser of the property hereby insured or herein described." (See also pages 44 and 84.)

ENDORSEMENTS.

(See also page 30.)

No endorsement carrying rebate, transfer, substitution or modification of form, or consent to assignment, shall be made on slips detached from the policy or certificate upon which the endorsement or consent to assignment is asked, but the policy or certificate shall in all such cases be presented to have the endorsement or consent made thereon, provided that temporary binders carrying the required endorsement or consent may be issued good for ten days, and each binder shall contain the following provision: "This endorsement or consent shall be void from and after 12 o'clock noon of the tenth day after this date unless also endorsed on the policy (or certificate)." See also page 31.)

EXCESS INSURANCE.

No reduction in rate shall be made for excess insurance, and if written it must be subject to the co-insurance conditions applying to the risk.

FIREWORKS.

Permits granting privilege to receive for shipment, or to store or keep fireworks for sale, shall be charged for in addition to the published rate, at the rate of $2\frac{1}{2}$ per cent. per annum, on the building and on the contents at the rate of 5 per cent. per annum, with short rates for shorter periods.

Chinese firecrackers and paper torpedoes in packages are not considered fireworks within the meaning of this rule.

FLOATING POLICIES.

No floating policy shall be written except under the exact form and at the rate adopted by the Board.

Provided that where the Board form will not properly cover the subject matter, a special form and rate may be promulgated, with the approval of the Executive Committee.

FORMS.

All forms adopted by the Board are mandatory from the respective dates of their adoption.

Unless written under the conditions governing blanket policies, insurance covering mills and manufactories shall be written specific so far as the following items are concerned:

$......on building; $......on machinery; $...... on boiler and engine; $......on stock; provided that when boiler and engine are in the main building they may be included in the machinery item (see also page 42); also insurance covering livery, boarding, sale and teaming stables and animals or other contents shall be written specific so far as the following items are concerned; $......on building; $......on animals (a limit to be fixed for loss on any one animal); $...... on vehicles and other contents.

A teaming stable within the meaning of this rule is one having accommodations for six horses or more and doing teaming. (See also pages 46 and 52.)

The commercial building form must be used in insuring brick commercial buildings other than preferred class within the jurisdiction of this Board. (For Form, see page 69.)

A commercial building within the meaning of this rule is one used or occupied wholly or in part for the sale or storage of goods, ware or merchandise or for office purposes or intended for such uses.

LEASEHOLD INTERESTS.

(See also page 41.)

Insurance of leasehold interests shall be subject to the same rates and rules as govern the writing of insurance on the building.

LUMBER, ETC.

(See also page 42.)

Insurance covering lumber or other property in sheds or yards when the property is separated into parts by open space or spaces of fifty feet or more, shall contain the average clause, unless written under the conditions governing blanket insurance.

MALT HOUSES.

(See also page 42.)

Insurance covering Malt Houses shall be written specifically as to the following items: $......on building; $...... on machinery, fixtures, furniture and tools; $......on stock.

OCCUPANCY.

(For form of occupancy clause, page 91.)

The use of any general clause carrying occupancy privileges except in cases where the policy covers merchandise or other personal property not in the hands of or under the immediate control of the assured is prohibited except it be under the following form: "Permission granted for the use of the premises as at present and for other purposes not any more hazardous, and to keep and use all articles and materials usual to the business conducted therein, but the use, handling, or storage of

a. Benzine,
b. Benzole,
c. Gasoline,
d. Naphtha,
e. Calcium Carbide or
f. Fireworks are prohibited unless a special permit is attached hereto."

When insurance is written on a risk upon which there is no specific published rate, no permit shall be granted for the occupancy of any part of the premises for any manufacturing or mechanical work, or for any other purpose than apartment houses, charitable institutions, churches, club houses, dwellings, flats, halls without scenery, offices, private boarding houses, private stables, public institutions, school houses, stores, basement and grade floor, together with dwellings, halls without scenery, offices or private boarding houses.

OPEN INSURANCE.

All insurance effected upon open entry shall be made subject to the conditions of what is known as the Standard Fire Insurance Policy of the State of New York, and to the payment of a full annual premium, in event of loss before being closed.

All open entries must be closed within thirty days after the date of the entry, and be closed on the basis of the rate existing at the time the insurance was made binding.

PATENT DEVICES.

A patent device committee, consisting of the Manager, Superintendents of Ratings and Chief Surveyor, may with the approval of the Executive Committee adopt rules governing the construction, installation and use of devices using crude petroleum or any of its lighter products for light, heat or power, or for any new device or material, the use of which will increase the fire hazard; and the Executive Committee may adopt forms of permit therefor, which when promulgated shall be binding on all members.

The rates and rules of the Board, in so far as they may affect any contract of insurance let by the State, the authorities of any Counties, city, town and village are advisory only.

RATE REDUCTIONS.

The making of improvements in a risk at the expense of a member or solicitor, the advancement of money to the assured to be subsequently repaid from a saving in the premium, or anything that results in cheapening insurance to the assured below the regular rate, is a valuable consideration granted him and a violation of the rates and rules of the Board.

REINSURANCE.

No member shall place reinsurance in any company which is represented in the City of Chicago by an agent doing a direct business and not a member of this Board.

The reinsurance of the whole or any part of a policy issued in contravention of any rate or rule of the Board, or by other than a member of the Board, is prohibited.

RETURNS AND ASSESSMENTS.

Assessments shall be due and payable upon presentation of bills therefor by the Secretary.

If returns are not made within thirty days after the expiration of the time provided in Section 14 of the Constitution, or assessments paid within thirty days after the assessment is levied, the Secretary shall make written demand therefor, and if returns are not made or assessment not paid within thirty days after written demand therefor by the Secretary, the delinquent member shall stand suspended, and business non-intercourse be declared against him.

SAFES AND VAULTS, property in:

For Form, see page 99.

SEPARATE SUBJECTS OF INSURANCE.

The following separate subjects of insurance when insured must each be insured specifically, and not covered together with any other subject:

1. Commissions on the sale of property of an agent, factor, merchant or other persons. (See also page 35.)
2. Common Carriers' Liability. (See also page 35.)
3. Consequential Damage. (See pages 35 and 70.)
4. Leasehold Interests. (See also page 39.)
5. Profits. (See also page 35.)
6. Rents and Rental Values. (For forms see pages 97-98.)
7. Sprinkler Leakage.
8. Storage Charges. (For form see page 101; see also page 43.)

9. Tornado Risks. (See also pages 49 and 54.)
10. Use and Occupancy. (For forms see page 113.)

The following are each separate subjects of insurance and insurance covering same must be written under a specific form of policy, or under the conditions governing blanket insurance:

1. (a) BREWERIES (see also page 32), building.
(b) Machinery, fixtures, furniture and tools therein.
(c) The stock and materials therefor.

2. (a) BUILDINGS, or subdivisions thereof, separated by fire walls, without openings, or with openings, when protected by fire doors or separated by open space, or iron storage tanks not housed. (See Buildings, page 32.)
(b) The contents—unless further restricted by rule—of each such building or subdivision. (See also page 36.)
(c) Parts of a building, improvements thereto or decorations thereof when insured for other than the owner of the building. (See also page 32.)

3. (a) COAL SHEDS (see also page 34), including the machinery and fixtures therein.
(b) Stock therein.
(c) The other movable personal property—except teaming outfit—for which see Stables, page 43.

4. ELECTRIC LIGHT AND POWER PLANTS. (See also page 37.)
(a) Building, including the boiler and engines.
(b) The motors, switchboards, dynamos, wiring and connections.
(c) The other contents of the building.

5. (a) ELEVATOR BUILDINGS (see also page 37), including machinery, fixtures and millwright work therein.
(b) The grain or other merchandise therein.

6. STORE FURNITURE AND FIXTURES in use, including electrical apparatus. (See also page 36.)

7. LUMBER or other property in sheds or yards when separated into two or more parts by open space of fifty feet or more, each part thereof is a separate subject of insurance. (See also pages 39 and 85.)

8. MACHINERY used in manufacturing, including tools, implements and apparatus. (See also page 33.)

9. (a) MALT HOUSES (see also page 39), BUILDING.
(b) MACHINERY, furniture, fixtures and tools therein.
(c) The stock and materials therefor.

10. MANUFACTORIES OR MILLS. See also page 39.)
(a) Building.
(b) Machinery.
(c) Boiler and engine (boiler and engine if in main building may be included with machinery).
(d) Stock.

11. MERCHANDISE IN STORES. (See also page 36.)
(b) Merchandise in storage warehouses, policy must exclude tobacco, unless the rate paid is the rate on tobacco.

12. STABLES, teaming livery and sale. (See also page 39.)
   (a) Building.
   (b) Animals.
   (c) Vehicles and other contents.

SPRINKLED RISKS. Maintenance Clause.

All policies covering risks where a reduction in rate has been granted for automatic sprinkler protection must contain the clause noted below, and the rate card and sheets must in all cases read: "Sprinkler maintenance clause required on all policies":

"Members shall not grant permission for any extensive alterations in or discontinuance of any sprinkler equipment for which allowance has been made in rate without the prior written approval of The Chicago Board of Underwriters."

For Sprinkler Maintenance Clause see page 110.

STORAGE CHARGES.

Insurance covering storage charges must be separately written under the Board form, and when so written rate charged must not be less than ninety per cent. of the contents rate. (See also page 41.)

For form for Storage Charges see page 101.

Freight advances and cartage may be included with storage charges.

TRANSFER OF INSURANCE.

Insurance may be transferred to cover the same property for the same owner in a new location when the property insured has been removed, or is being removed from one location to another, but not otherwise.

Insurance transferred from one location to another is subject to rate in the new location; and the difference in rate, if higher than in the old location, must be charged pro rata for the unexpired time of the insurance transferred, within thirty days from date of transfer; a pro rata rebate, if lower, may be paid.

Transfers covering in both old and new locations during removal must be made subject to the average clause, must be limited in time to not exceeding thirty days, and must provide that the insurance shall terminate in the old location at the end of thirty days. (For form of Removal Permit see page 97.)

When insurance is transferred from one location to another under the removal permit, the rate in the new location shall take effect from date of tranfser, whether it be higher or lower.

Whenever a policy is transferred from a place outside to a place inside of Cook County, where the rate is higher, additional premium pro rata of the difference in rate shall be collected for the unexpired time, and such transfers shall require the consent of an agent of the company having jurisdiction in the new location.

Whenever a policy is transferred into District Number One, either from outside Cook County or from District Number Two, it shall require the consent of a member of Class Number One.

WAREHOUSES.

Insurance shall not be written to cover the contents of more than one public storage warehouse under the same item.

Insurance covering property contained in any public storage warehouse may be transferred to cover the same property for the same owner in a new location where there is an actual removal of the property to such new location, but not otherwise; it shall not be assigned, and when cancelled it shall be at the usual short rates. It may contain a provision providing that the pledge of the property as collateral shall not make it invalid, and may have attached a clause making the loss payable to another, as follows: "Loss, if any, payable to .... or order hereon, but this insurance is void as to any subsequent owner or purchaser of the property hereby insured (or herein described).' (See also pages 37 and 101.)

WAIVER OF RIGHT OF SUBROGATION.

"Waiver of right of recovery under the subrogation clause of the policy shall not be granted in any case unless a waiver is authorized with the published rate, and the additional premium required to be charged for such waiver be charged and collected.

"The Superintendents of Ratings upon application therefor (and in other cases where they may deem it advisable) shall publish with the rate the additional charge to be made for such waiver, which additional charge shall not be less than 5 per cent of the published rate of the subject insured."

MINIMUM TARIFF

FOR PROPERTY <u>INSIDE</u> THE TERRITORY BOUNDED AS FOLLOWS:

Beginning at the intersection of Fullerton avenue with the Chicago River, thence east to Lake Michigan, thence southerly to Oakwood avenue, thence west to Ellis avenue, thence north to Thirty-ninth street, thence west to Halsted street, thence south to Forty-seventh street, thence west to Loomis street, thence north to Forty-fifth street, thence west to Ashland avenue, thence north to Thirty-ninth street, thence west to Western avenue, thence north to Illinois and Michigan Canal, thence westerly to West Fortieth avenue, thence north to West North avenue, thence east to Northwestern avenue, thence north to Belmont avenue, thence southerly along the north branch of the Chicago River to Fullerton avenue, at the place of beginning.

DWELLINGS.

	One Year.
Brick Dwellings and Contents	$0 30
Brick Dwellings and Contents written for a term of five years in no case less than 1 per cent.	
Single Frame Dwellings and Contents, detached not less than 50 feet in all directions	50
Single Frame Dwellings and Contents, detached not less than 25 feet in all directions	60
Single Frame Dwellings and Contents, detached 50 feet on one side	60
All other Frame Dwellings and Contents not less than	75
Brick Veneered Dwellings and Contents	40

Dwellings in part Brick and Frame shall rate as frame subject to survey and rating by the Board.

Dwellings Brick Veneered on all sides to be considered as brick dwellings in figuring exposures.

                 One Year.
Dwellings plastered outside, with tile or other non-combustible roof, and contents..........................$0 40

Brick Dwellings or Dwellings Brick Veneered on all sides, or Brick Buildings and Private Barns and Outbuildings on the same premises or in the rear of adjoining lots or buildings not considered as exposures.

 Streets, without reference to their width, to be considered as cutting off charge for exposure.

 Dwellings in which any mercantile or manufacturing business is carried on shall be treated as Mercantile Buildings under the Minimum Tariff unless special rates are applied for and promulgated by the Superintendent of Ratings, such published rates to be subject to his discretion.

STABLES AND OUTBUILDINGS.
                 One Year.
Brick Private Stables or Outbuildings and Contents......$0 30
Brick Private Stables or Outbuildings and Contents, written for a term of five years, in no case less than 1 per cent.
Single Private Frame Stables or Outbuildings and Contents, detached not less than 50 feet in all directions.. 50
Single Private Frame Stables or Outbuildings and Contents, detached not less than 25 feet in all directions.... 60
Single Private Frame Stables or Outbuildings and Contents, detached not less than 50 feet on one side........ 60
All other Private Frame Stables or Outbuildings and Contents 75
Brick Veneered Stables or Outbuildings and Contents...... 40
Stables or Outbuildings plastered outside, with tile or other non-combustible roof, and contents.................... 40

 Brick Stables or Outbuildings, or Stables or Outbuildings Brick Veneered on all sides, or Brick Buildings or Brick Dwellings not considered as exposures.

 Streets without reference to their width to be considered as cutting off charge for exposure.

 Stables, having accommodations for six or more horses, used for business purposes, shall be considered Special Hazards and MUST be rated by the Board before writing.

 Stables in part Brick and Frame shall rate as Frame, subject to survey and rating by the Board.

BRICK BUILDINGS AND CONTENTS, OCCUPIED FOR APARTMENT HOUSES OR FLATS, south of Harrison Street and north and west of the Chicago River.
                 One Year.
Three stories in height...........................$0 40
Four stories in height and 50 feet or less wide......... 50
Five stories in height and 50 feet or less wide.......... 60
Six stories or more in height and 50 feet or less wide.. 75

 Attics in buildings occupied for flats or apartment houses are not to be considered as additional stories.

Buildings three stories and over in height, occupied for dwelling purposes only, and having more than one tenant, are held to be buildings occupied for flats or apartment houses.

Buildings less than three stories in height, occupied for dwelling purposes only, with one or more tenants, are held to be dwellings.

All other flats or apartment houses must be specifically rated by the Board before writing.

BRICK BUILDINGS (other than apartment houses, churches, dwellings, schools, flats, buildings at Union Stock Yards and wood-working risks) in process of construction.

	One Year.
Two stories or less in height	$0 40
Three stories in height	50
Four stories in height	60
Five stories in height	75

Over five stories in height add 25 cents for each story.

Attics, in buildings occupied as stores below and dwellings above, are not to be considered as additional stories.

For rates on all buildings in process of construction at Union Stock Yards apply to Superintendent of Ratings.

BRICK BUILDINGS IN PROCESS OF CONSTRUCTION, south of Harrison Street and north and west of the Chicago River, with one or more of the following occupancies, which must always be stated in the policy, may be written for a longer term than one year:
(a) Charitable Institutions.
(b) Churches.
(c) Club Houses.
(d) Dwellings.
(e) Flats.
(f) Halls without scenery.
(g) Offices.
(h) Private Boarding Houses.
(i) Private Stables.
(j) Public Institutions.
(k) Schools.

All other buildings in process of construction must not be written for a longer term than one year.

BRICK BUILDINGS (other than apartment houses, churches, dwellings, flats and schools) not in process of construction, not rated.

	One Year.
Two stories or less in height	$0 40
Three stories in height	50
Four stories in height	60
Five stories in height	75

Over five stories in height add 25 cents for each story.

Attics, in buildings occupied as above, are not to be considered as additional stories.

BRICK BUILDINGS, not in process of construction not rated with one or more of the following occupancies, which must always be stated in the policy, may be written at the above minimum rates.
(a) Charitable Institutions.
(b) Club Houses.
(c) Halls without scenery.
(d) Offices.
(e) Private Boarding Houses.
(f) Public Institutions.

On all other buildings not in process of construction a rate must be published by the Board before insurance can be written.

SCHOOL HOUSES.

One Year.

Brick or Stone, with metal, slate or composition roof and contents $0 60
Brick or Stone, with shingle roof and contents............ 75
Frame and Contents..................................... 1 00

Brick Veneered and partly Brick and partly Frame shall rate same as Frame, unless specially rated by the Board.

CHURCHES.

One Year.

Brick or Stone and Contents.........................$ 0 75
Frame and Contents................................... 1 00

COAL YARDS.

Not to be written until specifically rated by the Board.

LUMBER YARDS.

Not to be written until specifically rated by the Board.

WOOD WORKING RISKS IN PROCESS OF CONSTRUCTION.

One Year.

Brick $1 50
Frame and Brick Veneered............................. 2 00

With Guaranty not to operate until specially rated.

FRAME COMMERCIAL BUILDINGS AND CONTENTS.

Brick Veneered Frame Buildings and Buildings partly Brick and partly Frame shall rate as Frame, subject to survey and rating by the Superintendent of Ratings.

One Year.

Frame Commercial Buildings detached 50 feet in all directions or exposed only by Brick Buildings or Brick Dwellings $1 00

	One Year.
Frame Commercial Buildings, detached 25 feet in all directions	1 25
On all other Frame Commercial Buildings the basis rate shall be	1 50

To this shall be added a charge for Exposures as follows:

Add 10 cents for each Frame Building in rows less than 25 feet apart up to 2½ per cent. It being understood that in rating Frame Commercial Buildings under the Tariff, ten (10) cents shall be added to the BASIS RATE of $1.50 for each street number as shown on the maps, half numbers not to be counted; provided that when buildings number on two streets, only one set of such numbers shall be used in making such rate, and when any building has more street numbers attached to it than it seems to be entitled to, the Superintendent of Ratings shall have the discretion in making the additions to rate called for by such street numbers; but no charge shall be added for Dwellings, Brick Buildings or Buildings Brick Veneered on ALL SIDES, and the same shall be considered as breaking the row.

From the rate so ascertained deduct 25 cents when the building to be insured stands on the corner of a street; is detached 50 feet or more on one side; or is exposed by Brick Buildings or Brick Dwellings.

Buildings composed in part of Brick and Frame shall be considered in figuring charges for exposures the same as Frame Buildings.

Buildings Brick Veneered on ALL SIDES to be considered as Brick Buildings in figuring exposures.

For specially hazardous exposures add at discretion.

Private Barns and Outbuildings on same premises or on rear of adjoining lots or buildings not occupied for specially hazardous or commercial purposes, not considered as exposures.

TORNADO OR CYCLONE INSURANCE.

	One Year.	Three Years.	Five Years.
1. Farm Property	$0 50	$0 75	$1 00
2. Cotton Gins, Elevators, Flouring Mills, Distilleries, Tobacco Stemmeries, prizing and rehandling houses and barns, Coal Shafts, Smelters, Salt Plants, Rolling Mills	50	75	1 00
3. Glass Factories	1 00	2 00	3 00
4. All other classes	20	40	60

NOTE.—Divisions 2 and 3 refer to ordinary brick or frame construction. When of fire proof, rates under Division 4 will apply.

TERM RATES.

Term rates on buildings south of Harrison Street and north and west of the Chicago River, occupied exclusively for one or more of the following purposes:

(a) Apartment Houses and Contents.
(b) Charitable Institutions and Contents.
(c) Churches and Contents.
(d) Club Houses and Contents.
(e) Dwellings and Contents.
(f) Flats and Furnished Rooms and Contents.
(g) Halls without Scenery and Contents.
(h) Offices and Contents.
(i) Private Boarding Houses and Contents.
(j) Private Stables and Contents.
(k) Public Institutions and Contents.
(l) Schools and Contents.
(m) One-story Buildings, Stores only, or Stores and Dwellings.
(n) Stores and Flats.
(o) Stores and Apartment Houses.
(p) Contents of Buildings described under (m), (n) and (o), except stocks.

    2 years 1½ annual rates.
    3 years 2 annual rates.
    4 years 2½ annual rates.
    5 years (except Brick Dwellings and Contents and Private Brick Stables and Contents) 3 annual rates.
    5 years Brick Dwellings and Contents, in no case less than 1 per cent.
    5 years Private Brick Stables, or Outbuildings and Contents, in no case less than 1 per cent.

When contents of mercantile buildings, other than furniture and fixtures, and other property not above specified, are written for more than one year, pro rata of the annual rate must be charged.

For term rates on other property than above see rate cards.

Policies covering merchandise cannot be written for a term exceeding fifteen months.

In applying the Minimum Tariff the Fire Maps shall be taken as the guide in ascertaining the Distances and Exposures.

MINIMUM TARIFF

FOR PROPERTY IN COOK COUNTY AND OUTSIDE THE TERRITORY BOUNDED AS FOLLOWS:

Beginning at the intersection of Fullerton avenue with the Chicago River, thence east to Lake Michigan, thence southerly to Oakwood avenue, thence west to Ellis avenue, thence north to Thirty-ninth street, thence west to Halsted street, thence south to Forty-seventh street, thence west to Loomis street, thence north to Forty-fifth street, thence west to Ashland avenue, thence north to Thirty-ninth street, thence west to Western avenue, thence north to Illinois and Michigan Canal, thence westerly to West Fortieth avenue, thence north to West North avenue, thence east to Northwestern avenue, thence north to Belmont avenue, thence southerly along the north branch of the Chicago River to Fullerton avenue, at the place of beginning.

DWELLINGS.

	One Year.
Brick Dwellings and Contents	$0 30
Brick Dwellings and Contents written for a term of five years in no case less than 1 per cent.	
Single Frame Dwellings and Contents, detached not less than 50 feet in all directions	50
Single Frame Dwellings and Contents, detached not less than 25 feet in all directions	60
Single Frame Dwellings and Contents, detached 50 feet on one side	60
All other Frame Dwellings and Contents not less than	75
Brick Veneered Dwellings and Contents	40
Dwellings plastered outside, with tile or other non-combustible roof, and Contents	40

Provided, however, that Frame Dwellings exposed by Frame Commercial Buildings or any Special Hazard within twenty-five (25) feet, shall rate the same as the highest rated exposure less a deduction of fifty cents, or seventy-five cents when the Dwelling to be rated is detached not less than fifty feet or exposed by a Brick Building on one side; subject to survey and rating by the Board where the exposure is of brick construction.

Dwellings in part Brick and Frame shall rate as frame, subject to survey and rating by the Board.

Brick Dwellings or Dwellings Brick Veneered on all sides or Brick Buildings and Private Barns and Outbuildings on the same premises or in the rear of adjoining lots or buildings, not considered as exposures.

Streets, without reference to their width, to be considered as cutting off charge for exposure.

Dwellings in which any mercantile or manufacturing business is carried on shall be treated as Mercantile Buildings under the Minimum Tariff unless a special rate is applied for and promulgated by the Superintendent of Ratings, such published rates to be subject to his discretion.

STABLES AND OUTBUILDINGS.

	One Year.
Brick Private Stables or Outbuildings and Contents	$0.30
Brick Private Stables or Outbuildings and Contents, written for a term of five years, in no case less than 1 per cent.	
Single Private Frame Stables or Outbuildings and Contents, detached not less than 50 feet in all directions	50
Single Private Frame Stables or Outbuildings and Contents, detached not less than 25 feet in all directions	60
Single Private Frame Stables or Outbuildings and Contents, detached not less than 50 feet on one side	60
All other Private Frame Stables or Outbuildings and Contents	75
Brick Veneered Stables or Outbuildings and Contents	40
Stables or Outbuildings, plastered outside, with tile or other non-combustible roof, and contents	40

Provided, however, that Frame Stables or Outbuildings exposed by Frame Commercial Buildings, or any Special Hazard within twenty-five (25) feet, shall rate the same as the highest rated exposure less a deduction of fifty cents or seventy-five cents when the Stable or Outbuilding to be rated is detached not less than fifty feet or exposed by a Brick Building on one side; subject to survey and rating by the Board, where the exposure is of brick construction.

Brick Stables or Outbuildings, or Stables or Outbuildings Brick Veneered on all sides, or Brick Buildings or Brick Dwellings not considered as exposures.

Streets, without reference to their width, to be considered as cutting off charge for exposure.

Stables, having accommodations for six or more horses, used for business purposes, shall be considered Special Hazards and MUST be rated by the Board before writing.

Stables in part Brick and Frame shall rate as Frame, subject to survey and rating by the Board.

BRICK BUILDINGS AND CONTENTS, OCCUPIED FOR APARTMENT HOUSES OR FLATS.

One Year.

Three stories in height	$0 40
Four stories in height and 50 feet or less wide	50
Five stories in height and 50 feet or less wide	60
Six stories or more in height and 50 feet or less wide	75

Attics in buildings occupied for flats or apartment houses are not to be considered as additional stories.

Buildings, three stories and over in height, occupied for dwelling purposes only, and having more than one tenant, are held to be buildings occupied for flats or apartment houses.

Buildings less than three stories in height, occupied for dwelling purposes only, with one or more tenants, are held to be dwellings.

All other flats or apartment houses must be specifically rated by the Board before writing.

SCHOOL HOUSES.

One Year.

Brick or Stone with metal, slate or composition roof and contents	$0 60
Brick or Stone, with shingle roof and contents	75
Frame and contents	1 00

Brick Veneered and partly Brick and partly Frame shall rate same as Frame, unless specially rated by the Board.

CHURCHES.

One Year.

Brick or Stone and Contents	$0 75
Frame and Contents	1 00

COAL YARDS.

Not to be written until specifically rated by the Board.

LUMBER YARDS.

Not to be written until specifically rated by the Board.

WOOD WORKING RISKS AND ALL OTHER SPECIAL HAZARDS in Process of Construction.

One Year.

Brick	$1 50
Frame and Brick Veneered	2 00

With Guaranty not to operate until specially rated.

TORNADO OR CYCLONE INSURANCE.

	One Year.	Three Years.	Five Years.
1. Farm Property	$0 50	$0 75	$1 00
2. Cotton Gins, Elevators, Flouring Mills, Distilleries, Tobacco Stemmeries, prizing and rehandling houses and barns, Coal Shafts, Smelters, Salt Plants, Rolling Mills	50	75	1 00
3. Glass Factories	1 00	2 00	3 00
4. All other classes	20	40	60

NOTE.—Divisions 2 and 3 refer to ordinary brick or frame construction. When of fire proof, rates under Division 4 will apply.

SECTION ONE.

The following tariff applies to all that section bounded by Seventy-first Street on the south, South Forty-eighth Avenue and North Forty-eighth Avenue on the west, to Devon Avenue, east on Devon Avenue to North Kedzie Avenue, north on North Kedzie Avenue to Howard Avenue, east on Howard Avenue to Lake Michigan, including risks on both sides of the above named streets and avenues.

BRICK BUILDINGS (other than apartment houses, churches, dwellings, flats, schools, wood working risks, and other special hazards) in process of construction.

	One Year.
Two stories or less in height	$0 40
Three stories in height	50
Four stories in height	60
Five stories in height	75

Over five stories in height add 25 cents for each story.

Attics in buildings occupied as stores below and dwellings above, are not to be considered as additional stories.

Buildings in process of construction, with one or more of the following occupancies, which must always be stated in the policy, may be written for a longer term than one year.
(a) Charitable Institutions.
(b) Churches.
(c) Club Houses.
(d) Dwellings.
(e) Flats.
(f) Halls without scenery.
(g) Offices.
(h) Private Boarding Houses.
(i) Private Stables.
(j) Public Institutions.
(k) Schools.

All other buildings in process of construction must not be written for a longer term than one year.

BRICK BUILDINGS (other than apartment houses, churches, dwellings, flats and schools) not in process of construction, not rated.

　　　　　　　　　　　　　　　　　　　　　　　　One Year.
Two stories or less in height..........................$0 40
Three stories in height................................. 50
Four stories in height.................................. 60
Five stories in height.................................. 75

Over five stories in height add 25 cents for each story.

Attics, in buildings occupied as above, are not to be considered as additional stories.

Buildings not in process of construction not rated with one or more of the following occupancies, which must always be stated in the policy, may be written at the above minimum rates.

(a) Charitable Institutions.
(b) Club Houses.
(c) Halls without scenery.
(d) Offices.
(e) Private Boarding Houses.
(f) Public Institutions.

On all other buildings a rate must be published by the Board before insurance can be written.

CONTENTS.

All Contents, including Household Furniture, of Brick Buildings other than Dwellings, rate 25 cents more than Building.

FRAME COMMERCIAL BUILDINGS AND CONTENTS.

Brick Veneered Frame Buildings and Buildings partly Brick and partly Frame shall rate as Frame, subject to survey and rating by the Superintendent of Ratings.

　　　　　　　　　　　　　　　　　　　　　　　　One Year.
Frame Commercial Buildings detached 50 feet in all directions or exposed only by Brick Buildings or Brick Dwellings $1 25
Frame Commercial Buildings, detached 25 feet in all directions 1 50
On all other Frame Commercial Buildings the basis rate shall be. 1 75

To the basis rate of $1.75 additional charges shall be made for exposures, as follows:

For all Frame Commercial Buildings standing less than twenty-five (25) feet apart in any direction from risk, add ten (10) cents for each building, but no charge shall be added for Dwellings built for and occupied exclusively as such.

Brick Commercial Buildings or Buildings Brick Veneered on all sides shall be considered as breaking the Frame Row in which they are situated.

From the rate so ascertained, 25 cents may be deducted when the Building to be insured is detached fifty (50) feet or more on one side or is exposed by Brick Veneered Commercial Buildings or Brick Dwellings.

It is, however, understood that the above basis for rating does not apply where any special or manufacturing hazard is within exposing distance of the risks to be rated, but in such cases such extra rates shall be applied as the judgment of the Superintendent of Ratings may determine.

It is further understood that each ground floor occupant having twenty-five (25) feet or less, shall rate as one building, and where one occupant has over twenty-five (25) feet of grade frontage, the risk shall rate as one building for each twenty-five (25) feet or any part thereof.

It is further understood that the Contents of all Frame Buildings rated as provided above shall bear the same rate as the Building.

Buildings composed in part of Brick and Frame shall be considered in figuring charges for exposures the same as Frame buildings.

Private Barns and Outbuildings on same premises, or on rear of adjoining lots or buildings, not occupied for specially hazardous or commercial purposes, not considered as exposures.

SECTION TWO.

The following tariff applies to all of Cook County outside of territory described in Section One.

BRICK BUILDINGS (other than apartment houses, churches, dwellings, flats, schools, wood working risks, and other special hazards) in process of construction.

	One Year.
Two stories or less in height	$0 50
Three stories in height	60
Four stories in height	75
Five stories in height	1 00

Over five stories in height add 25 cents for each story.

Attics, in buildings occupied as stores below and dwellings above, are not to be considered additional stories.

Buildings in process of construction with one or more of the following occupancies, which must be always stated in the policy, may be written for a longer term than one year:
(a) Charitable Institutions.
(b) Churches.
(c) Club Houses.
(d) Dwellings.
(e) Flats.
(f) Halls without scenery.
(g) Offices.
(h) Private Boarding Houses.
(i) Private Stables.
(j) Public Institutions.
(k) Schools.

All other buildings in process of construction must not be written for a longer term than one year.

BRICK BUILDINGS (other than apartment houses, churches, dwellings, flats and schools) not in process of construction, not rated.

                       One Year.
Two stories or less in height.................................$0 50
Three stories in height................................... 60
Four stories in height.................................... 75
Five stories in height.................................... 1 00
  Over five stories in height add 25 cents for each story.

  Attics, in buildings occupied as above are not to be considered as additional stories.

  Buildings not in process of construction, not rated with one or more of the following occupancies, which must always be stated in the policy, may be written at the above minimum rates.

(a) Charitable Institutions.
(b) Club Houses.
(c) Halls without scenery.
(d) Offices.
(e) Private Boarding Houses.
(f) Public Institutions.

  On all other buildings a rate must be published by the Board before insurance can be written.

CONTENTS.

  All Contents, including Household Furniture, of Brick Buildings other than Dwellings, rate 25 cents more than building.

FRAME COMMERCIAL BUILDINGS AND CONTENTS.

  Brick Veneered Frame Buildings, and Buildings partly Brick and partly Frame, shall rate as Frame, subject to survey and rating by the Superintendent of Ratings.

                       One Year.
Frame Commercial Buildings detached 50 feet in all directions or exposed only by Brick Buildings or Brick Dwellings $1 50
Frame Commercial Buildings, detached 25 feet in all directions 1 75
On all other Frame Commercial Buildings the basis rate shall be... 1 75

  To the basis rate of $1.75 additional charges shall be made for exposures, as follows:

  For all Frame Commercial Buildings standing less than twenty-five (25) feet apart in any direction from risk, add 25 cents for each building up to six per cent, but no charge shall be added for Dwellings built for and occupied exclusively as such.

  Brick Commercial Buildings or Buildings Brick Veneered on all sides shall be considered as breaking the Frame Row in which they are situated.

It is, however, understood that the foregoing basis of rating does not apply where any Special or Manufacturing Hazard is within exposing distance of the risks to be rated, but in such cases such extra rates shall be applied as the judgment of the Superintendent of Ratings may determine.

It is further understood that each ground floor occupant having twenty-five (25) feet or less shall rate as one building, and where one occupant has over twenty-five (25) feet of grade frontage, the risk shall rate as one building for each twenty-five (25) feet or any part thereof.

It is further understood that the contents of all Frame Buildings rated as provided above, shall bear the same rate as the building.

Buildings composed in part of Brick and Frame, shall be considered in figuring charges for exposures the same as Frame Buildings.

Private Barns and Outbuildings on same premises, or on rear of adjoining lots or buildings not occupied for specially hazardous or commercial purposes, not considered as exposures.

For Rates on all other Brick Commercial and Frame Commercial Buildings and on property where the foregoing does not apply application must be made to the Board.

FARM PROPERTY.

	One Year.	Three Years.	Five Years.
Dwellings, Barns, Outbuildings and Contents when written under same Policy.	$0 50	$1 00	$1 50
Where Farm Barns and Contents are written without the Dwelling............	75	1 50	2 25

Farm property is defined as follows: The words Farm Property shall be understood to mean farm buildings and their contents located on farms occupied only for farming purposes, and shall not be understood as covering or applying to any building or property located within any city or incorporated village, however remote from other buildings they may be.

TERM RATES.

Term rates on buildings occupied exclusively for one or more of the following purposes:
(a) Apartment Houses and Contents.
(b) Charitable Institutions and Contents.
(c) Churches and Contents.
(d) Club Houses and Contents.
(e) Dwellings and Contents.
(f) Flats and Furnished Rooms and Contents.
(g) Halls without Scenery and Contents.
(h) Offices and Contents.
(i) Private Boarding Houses and Contents.
(j) Private Stables and Contents.

(k) Public Institutions and Contents.
(l) Schools and Contents.
(m) One-story Buildings, Stores only, or Stores and Dwellings.
(n) Stores and Flats.
(o) Stores and Apartment Houses.
(p) Contents of Buildings described under (m), (n) and (c), except stocks:

2 years 1½ annual rates.
3 years 2 annual rates.
4 years 2½ annual rates.
5 years (except brick dwellings and contents and private brick stables and contents) 3 annual rates.
5 years brick dwellings and contents, in no case less than 1 per cent.
5 years private brick stables, or outbuildings and contents, in no case less than 1 per cent.

When contents of mercantile buildings other than furniture and fixtures, and other property not above specified, are written for more than one year, pro rata of the annual rate must be charged.

For term rates on other property than above see rate sheets.

Policies covering merchandise cannot be written for a term exceeding fifteen months.

In applying the Minimum Tariff the Fire Maps shall be taken as the guide in ascertaining the Distances and Exposures.

APARTMENT HOUSES are buildings more than 50 feet wide and more than three stories high, occupied for dwelling purposes only, having more than one tenant.

FLATS are buildings 50 feet or less wide and three stories and over high, occupied for dwelling purposes only, having more than one tenant.

STORES AND APARTMENT HOUSES are buildings more than 50 feet wide and more than three stories high, occupied for stores, basement and grade floor only, dwellings, halls without scenery, offices and private boarding houses.

STORES AND FLATS are buildings 50 feet or less wide and three stories and over high, occupied for stores, basement and grade floor only, dwellings, halls without scenery, offices and private boarding houses.

FORMS

FORM OF PERMIT FOR ACETYLENE GAS.

Adopted January 11th, 1906.

See also page 30.

Permission may be granted for the generation and use of Acetylene Gas under the following form, but not otherwise:

PERMIT FOR THE USE OF ACETYLENE GAS.

In consideration of the following warranties on the part of the assured, permission is hereby granted to generate and use acetylene gas on the premises described in this policy, using a ....Acetylene Gas Machine manufactured by ....
at ....

The use of Liquid Acetylene or Gas generated therefrom on the premises described herein is absolutely prohibited.

WARRANTED.

1. That the charging of the generator or the handling of calcium carbide shall be by daylight only.
2. That no artificial light shall be permitted within ten (10) feet, and that no fire shall be permitted within fifteen (15) feet of the generator.
3. That no calcium carbide, except that contained in the generator, shall be kept in the building where this policy covers.
4. That no additions to or changes in the installation shall be made without notice to and the written consent of this company endorsed hereon.

CAUTIONS.

1. Calcium Carbide should be kept in water-tight metal cans, by itself, outside of any insured building, under lock and key and where it is not exposed to the weather.
2. A regular time should be set for attending to and charging the apparatus during daylight hours only.
3. In charging generating chambers, clean all residuum carefully from the containers and remove it at once from the building. Separate the unexhausted carbide, if any, from the mass and return it to the container, adding new carbide as required. Be careful never to fill the container over the specified mark, as it is important to allow for the swelling of the carbide when it comes in contact with water. The proper action and economy of the machine is dependent on the arrangement and amount of carbide placed in the generator. Carefully guard against the escape of gas.
4. Whenever recharging with carbide, always replenish water supply.

5. Never deposit the residuum or exhausted material in the sewer pipes or near inflammable material.

6. Water tanks and water seals must always be kept filled with clean water.

7. Never install more than the equivalent of the number of half-foot burners for which the machine is rated.

8. Never test the generator or piping for leaks with a flame, and never apply flame to an outlet from which the burner has been removed.

9. Never use a lighted match, lamp, candle, lantern or any open light near the machine.

10. See that the installation is in accordance with the rules of The Chicago Board of Underwriters, a copy of which may be obtained of your insurance agent, and obtain a written guarantee from the party installing same that these rules have been complied with.

E. A. ARMSTRONG MFG. CO. FLOATER.

$........On merchandise in the hands of others subject to purchase or return, and on merchandise and materials therefor in the hands of others for manufacture, while contained in any building except a storage warehouse and except the premises of the assured in Cook County, Ill.

In consideration of the rate at which this policy is written it is expressly stipulated and made a condition of this contract that this company shall be liable for no greater proportion of any loss than the amount hereby insured bears to eighty per cent. of the actual cash value of the property described herein at the time when such loss shall happen, nor for more than the proportion which this policy bears to the total contributing insurance thereon. If this policy be divided into two or more items, the foregoing conditions shall apply to each item separately.

But it is at the same time declared and agreed, that if any specific parcel of goods included in the terms of this policy or such goods in any specified building or buildings, place or places, within the limits of this insurance, shall at the time of any fire be insured in this or any other company, this policy shall not extend to cover the same excepting only as far as relates to any excess of value beyond the amount of such specific insurance, and shall not be liable for any loss, unless the amount of such loss shall exceed the amount of such specific insurance, (disregarding the liability of the assured as an insurer under any co-insurance clause under such specific insurance,) which said excess only is declared to be under the protection of this policy and subject to average aforesaid. It being the true intent and meaning of this agreement that this company shall not be liable for any loss, unless the amount of such loss shall exceed the amount of specific insurance, and then only for such excess, which said excess shall be subject to average as above.

Other insurance permitted.

Form No. 1.—Floater for Electric Automobiles.

Adopted January 11, 1906.

Rate under this form, 1 per cent. Advance does not apply.

$........On Automobile No......made by...............
propelled by an electric motor, and on its equipment, while within the limits of Cook County, Illinois, either in or out of building or on road.

It is hereby stipulated that the risk assumed by this company is against fire originating outside of the machine, and that no claim shall be made for loss or damage by fire originating in or on the machine itself.

It is understood and agreed that this insurance does not cover any loss or damage to electrical machinery, apparatus or connections caused by electric currents, whether artificial or natural.

Form No. 2.—Floater for Electric Automobiles.

Adopted January 11, 1906.

Rate under this form, 1¼ per cent. Advance does not apply.

$........On Automobile No......made by...............
propelled by an electric motor, and on its equipment, while within the limits of Cook County, Illinois, either in or out of building or on the road.

It is understood and agreed that this insurance does not cover any loss or damage to electrical machinery, apparatus or connections caused by electric currents, whether artificial or natural.

Form No. 3.—Floater for Electric Automobiles.

Adopted January 11, 1906.

Rate under this form, 1¼ per cent. Advance does not apply.

$........On Automobile No......made by...............
propelled by an electric motor, and on its equipment, while within the limits of the United States or Canada, either in or out of building, on road, or being transported by rail, by inland vessel, or on any coastwise vessel bound from any United States or Canadian port to another.

It is hereby stipulated that the risk assumed by this company is against fire originating outside of the machine, and that no claim shall be made for loss or damage by fire originating in or on the machine itself.

It is understood and agreed that this insurance does not cover any loss or damage to electrical machinery, apparatus or connections caused by electric currents, whether artificial or natural.

Form No. 4.—Floater for Electric Automobiles.

Adopted January 11, 1906.

Rate under this form, 1½ per cent. Advance does not apply.

$........On Automobile No......made by................ propelled by an electric motor, and on its equipment, while within the limits of the United States or Canada, either in or out of building, on road, or being transported by rail, by inland vessel, or on any coastwise vessel bound from any United States or Canadian port to another.

It is understood and agreed that this insurance does not cover any loss or damage to electrical machinery, apparatus or connections caused by electric currents, whether artificial or natural.

Form No. 1.—Permit for Automobiles Using Gasoline.

Adopted January 11, 1906

Rate for this permit, 25 cents for one Automobile, and 5 cents for each additional Automobile.

In consideration of $..........additional premium, and the compliance of the assured with the hereinafter named warranty, permission is hereby given to keep not more than............ automobiles using gasoline for fuel or power, in the building described in this policy; it being a condition of this permit that this insurance excludes any loss or damage to an automobile, any of its parts or its contents, insured under this policy, caused by fire originating in the automobile itself.

It is warranted by the assured that the refilling of the reservoir of an automobile, while the same is contained in the within insured building, shall take place by daylight only; that no fire, blaze or artificial light, other than incandescent electric light, shall be permitted in the room where and when the said reservoir is being filled; that no gasoline except such as is contained in said reservoir or reservoirs shall be kept within the said building, and that all excess of gasoline over that contained in the said reservoir or reservoirs shall be kept outside of said building.

Form No. 2.—Permit for Automobiles Using Gasoline.

Adopted January 11, 1906.

Rate for this permit, 50 cents for one Automobile, and 5 cents for each additional Automobile.

In consideration of $..........additional premium, and the compliance of the assured with the hereinafter named warranty, permission is hereby given to keep not more than............ automobiles using gasoline for fuel or power, in the building described in this policy.

It is warranted by the assured that the refilling of the reservoir of an automobile, while the same is contained in the within

insured building, shall take place by daylight only; that no fire, blaze or artificial light, other than incandescent electric light, shall be permitted in the room where and when the said reservoir is being filled; that no gasoline except such as is contained in said reservoir or reservoirs in excess of five gallons shall be kept within the said building.

Form No. 1.—Floater for Automobiles Using Gasoline.

Adopted January 11, 1906.

Rate under this form, 1¼ per cent. Advance does not apply.

$........On Automobile No.......made by...............
propelled by a gasoline or steam motor, and on its equipment, while within the limits of Cook County, Ill., either in or out of building or while on road.

It is hereby stipulated that the risk assumed by this company is limited to fire originating outside of the machine, and that no claim shall be made for loss or damage by fire originating in or on the machine itself.

Warranted by the assured that when any building in which the machine may be located is owned or controlled by the assured, no gasoline, naphtha or other light product of petroleum (other than that in the car tank), shall be stored in the same building with the car.

Form No. 2.—Floater for Automobiles Using Gasoline.

Adopted January 11, 1906.

Rate under this form, 1¾ per cent. Advance does not apply.

$........On Automobile No. ...... made by...............
propelled by a gasoline or steam motor, and on its equipment, while within the limits of Cook County, Ill., either in or out of building or while on road.

Warranted by the assured that when any building in which the machine may be located is owned or controlled by the assured, no gasoline, naphtha or other light product of petroleum (other than that in the car tank), shall be stored in the same building with the car.

Form No. 3.—Floater for Automobiles Using Gasoline.

Adopted January 11th, 1906.

Rate under this form, 1½ per cent. Advance does not apply.

$........On Automobile No......made by...............
propelled by a gasoline or steam motor, and on its equipment, while within the limits of the United States or Canada, either in or out of building, on road or being transported by rail, by inland vessel, or on any coastwise vessel bound from one United States or Canadian port to another.

It is hereby stipulated that the risk assumed by this company is limited to fire originating outside of the machine, and that no claim shall be made for loss or damage by fire originating in or on the machine itself.

Warranted by the assured that when any building in which the machine may be located is owned or controlled by the assured, no gasoline, naphtha or other light product of petroleum (other than that in the car tank) shall be stored in the same building with the car.

Form No. 4.—Floater for Automobiles Using Gasoline.

Adopted January 11th, 1906.

Rate under this form, 2 per cent. Advance does not apply.

$........On Automobile No......made by................ propelled by a gasoline or steam motor, and on its equipment, while within the limits of the United States or Canada, either in or out of building, on road or being transported by rail, by inland vessel, or on any coastwise vessel bound from one United States or Canadian port to another.

Warranted by the assured that when any building in which the machine may be located is owned or controlled by the assured, no gasoline, naphtha or other light product of petroleum (other than that in the car tank) shall be stored in the same building with the car.

AVERAGE CLAUSE.—Building.

Adopted January 11th, 1906.

See also page 30.

This Policy to attach on each building in proportion as the value of each bears to the value of all.

AVERAGE CLAUSE.—Contents of Buildings.

Adopted January 11th, 1906.

See also page 30.

This Policy to attach in each building in proportion as the value of each bears to the value of all.

AVERAGE CLAUSE.—Location or Division.

Adopted January 11th, 1906.

See also page 30.

NOTE.—To be used on Policies insuring lumber yards, coal yards or other property where the rules provide that open spaces of 50 feet or more create separate subjects of insurance.

This Policy to attach in each location or division in proportion as the value in each bears to the value in all.

BAGS AND BAGGING.—Floater.

Adopted January 11th, 1906.

Rate under this form, 3 per cent. Advance applies.

$........On Bags and Bagging, their own, or held by them in trust or on commission, or sold but not delivered, while contained in any printing establishment, laundry or dry room, excepting the premises of the assured, and while contained in any freight house or in cars on tracks, or in transit in Cook County, Illinois, when at the risk of the assured.

It is hereby declared and agreed that in case the property aforesaid in all the buildings, places or limits included in this insurance, shall, at the breaking out of any fire or fires, be collectively of greater value than the sum insured, then this company shall pay and make good such portion only of the loss or damage as the sum hereby insured shall bear to the whole value of the property aforesaid at the time when such fire or fires shall first happen.

But, it is at the same time declared and agreed, that if any specific property described above included in the terms of this policy, shall at the time of any fire be insured in this or any other company, this policy shall not extend to cover the same, excepting only as far as relates to any excess of value beyond the amount of such specific insurance, and shall not be liable for any loss unless the amount of such loss shall exceed the amount of such specific insurance, which said excess only is declared to be under the protection of this policy and subject to average aforesaid.

Other insurance permitted without notice until required.

BUILDING EQUIPMENT FLOATER—(Elevators).

Adopted January 11th, 1906.

Rate under this form, $1.75. Advance applies.

$........On elevators, parts thereof, materials therefor, and tools, implements, and appliances used in constructing same, their own or in which they may have an interest, or for which they may be liable, while contained in any building except a storage warehouse, and except the premises of the assured in Cook County, Illinois.

In consideration of the rate at which this policy is written it is expressly stipulated and made a condition of this contract that this company shall be liable for no greater proportion of any loss than the amount hereby insured bears to the actual cash value of the property described herein at the time when such loss shall happen, nor for more than the proportion which this policy bears to the total contributing insurance thereon.

But, it is at the same time declared and agreed, that if any specific property described above included in the terms of this policy, shall at the time of any fire be insured in this or any other

company, this policy shall not extend to cover the same, excepting only as far as relates to any excess of value beyond the amount of such specific insurance, and shall not be liable for any loss unless the amount of such loss shall exceed the amount of such specific insurance (disregarding the liability of the assured as an insurer under any co-insurance clause, under such specific insurance), which said excess only is declared to be under the protection of this policy and subject to average aforesaid.

Other insurance permitted.

This insurance does not cover any loss or damage to electric machinery, apparatus and connections, caused by electric currents, whether artificial or natural.

BUILDING NON-OCCUPANCY CLAUSE.

Adopted January 11th, 1906.

See also page 33.

NOTE.—When a policy is written on an unoccupied building having a published, specific rate, or when a rate is reduced for non-occupancy and a rebate is allowed, the following form is to be used:

The premium charged herefor being for the hazard of the building unoccupied, it is understood and agreed that when occupied in whole or in part, notice shall be given to this Company at once, and payment made of additional premium, if any, required to cover the hazard of such occupancy.

PERMIT FOR STORAGE OF CALCIUM CARBIDE CONTAINED IN METAL CANS NOT EXCEEDING TWO POUNDS EACH.

Adopted January 11th, 1906.

See also page 33.

In consideration of the following warranties on the part of the assured permission is hereby granted to store not exceeding one hundred (100) pounds of Calcium Carbide on the premises described in this policy.

WARRANTED.

1. That all calcium carbide will be contained in water-tight metal cans having a capacity not exceeding two pounds each.

2. That all such metal cans of calcium carbide will be stored in a magazine or holder constructed in accordance with the specifications printed hereon.

3. That all calcium carbide will be stored above the grade of the street.

SPECIFICATIONS FOR MAGAZINES OR HOLDERS.

To be constructed of galvanized iron with all seams lapped, riveted and soldered both inside and out so as to form thoroughly water-tight joints.

Bottoms to be raised at least six inches from floor by legs or rims.

Must have cover which, when closed, will form a water-tight joint, and all removable parts must be securely attached to the holder by some efficient device, such as a chain.

Must be so that not more than fifty (50) two-pound packages can be placed in any one holder.

Must be plainly marked in letters at least two inches in height, "Calcium Carbide—Keep Dry," and cover must be marked "Keep Closed."

NOTE.—Detailed specifications for the construction of approved holders as adopted by The Chicago Board of Underwriters can be obtained of your insurance agent.

CHICAGO EMBROIDERING AND BRAIDING CO.—Floater.

Adopted January 11, 1906.

Rate under this form, 2 per cent. Advance applies.

$........On merchandise consisting chiefly of laces, embroideries, garments and materials therefor, their own or in which they may have an interest, or for which they may be liable while contained in any building except a storage warehouse and except the premises of the assured, in Cook County, Illinois.

In consideration of the rate at which this policy is written it is expressly stipulated and made a condition of this contract that this company shall be liable for no greater proportion of any loss than the amount hereby insured bears to the actual cash value of the property described herein at the time when such loss shall happen, nor for more than the proportion which this policy bears to the total contributing insurance thereon.

But it is at the same time declared and agreed that if any specific property described above, included in the terms of this policy, shall at the time of any fire be insured in this or any other company, this policy shall not extend to cover the same, excepting only as far as relates to any excess of value beyond the amount of such specific insurance, and shall not be liable for any loss unless the amount of such loss shall exceed the amount of such specific insurance (disregarding the liability of the assured as an insurer under any co-insurance clause, under such specific insurance), which said excess only is declared to be under the protection of this policy and subject to average aforesaid.

Other insurance permitted without notice until required.

It is understood and agreed that this company shall not be liable for an amount exceeding 20 per cent of the amount of this policy for loss by any one fire.

CATERING HOUSE FLOATER.
Adopted February 26th, 1907.
Rate 2 per cent. Advance applies.

$..........On its furniture, furnishings, tools, implements, utensils, and food, used in serving meals and luncheon elsewhere than on its own premises, while contained in any building except storage warehouses, and except the premises of the assured in Cook County, Illinois.

It is a part of the consideration for this policy and the basis upon which the rate of premium is fixed, that the assured shall maintain insurance upon the property described by this policy to the extent of the actual cash value thereof and that failing so to do the assured shall be an insurer to the extent of such deficit, and to that extent shall bear his, her or their proportion of any loss.

But it is at the same time declared and agreed, that if any specific property described above, included in the terms of this policy, shall, at the time of any fire, be insured in this or any other company, this policy shall not extend to cover the same, excepting only as far as relates to any excess of value beyond the amount of such specific insurance, and shall not be liable for any loss unless the amount of such loss shall exceed the amount of such specific insurance (disregarding the liability of the assured as an insurer under any co-insurance clause, under such specific insurance) which said excess only is declared to be under the protection of this policy and subject to average aforesaid.

Other insurance permitted.

It is understood and agreed that this company shall not be liable for an amount exceeding its proportion of $1,000 for loss by any one fire.

THE CHICAGO LAW INSTITUTE.—Floater.

Adopted January 11, 1906.

Rate under this form, 3 per cent. Advance applies.

$........On merchandise, consisting chiefly of books in the hands of others, whether manufactured or in process of manufacture or being repaired and the materials therefor, their own or held by them in trust, or for which they are legally liable in case of loss by fire, while contained in any building in Cook County, Illinois, except all storage warehouses and except the premises of the assured.

It is a part of the consideration for this policy and the basis upon which the rate of premium is fixed that the assured shall maintain insurance upon the property described by this policy, to the extent of the actual cash value thereof, and that, failing so to do, the assured shall be an insurer to the extent of such deficit, and to that extent shall bear his, her or their proportion of any loss.

But it is at the same time declared and agreed that if any specific property described above, included in the terms of this policy, shall at the time of any fire be insured in this or any other company, this policy shall not extend to cover the same, excepting only as far as relates to any excess of value beyond the amount of such specific insurance, and shall not be liable for any loss unless the amount of such loss shall exceed the amount of such specific insurance (disregarding the liability of the assured as an insurer under any co-insurance clause, under such specific insurance), which said excess only is declared to be under the protection of this policy and subject to average aforesaid.

Other insurance permitted.

It is understood and agreed that this company shall not be liable for an amount exceeding its pro rata part of $1,000 for loss by any one fire.

COMMERCIAL BUILDING FORM.

Adopted January 11, 1906.

See also page 39.

$......On the ......story........................building, its sidewalks, plate glass, boilers, engines, permanent fixtures, machinery pertaining to the service of the building, or furnishing power therein, but excluding any manufacturing apparatus or machinery, situate..
....
....
....
....

It is understood and agreed that the foundations of the building below the level of the under surface of the lowest basement floor are not insured under this policy.

It is understood and agreed that this insurance does not cover any loss or damage to electrical machinery, apparatus and

FORM FOR COMMON CARRIERS LIABILITY.
Adopted January 11, 1906
Rate, Contents Rate.

$......On their legal liability for Baggage Wares and Merchandise of others in their possession as Common Carriers while contained in..............................

Other insurance permitted.

connections caused by electric currents, whether artificial or natural.

Permission to make ordinary alterations and repairs.

Other insurance permitted.

COMPRESSED AIR HOUSE CLEANING MACHINES.—
Floater Form.
Adopted January 11, 1906.

Rate 4 per cent. Advance applies.

On Compressed Air House Cleaning Machines and contents of same while on streets and in open yards in Cook County, Illinois.

In consideration of the rate at which this policy is written it is expressly stipulated and made a condition of this contract that this company shall be liable for no greater proportion of any loss than the amount hereby insured bears to the actual cash value of the property described herein at the time when such loss shall happen, nor for more than the proportion which this policy bears to the total contributing insurance thereon.

But it is at the same time declared and agreed that if any specific property described above, included in the terms of this policy, shall at the time of any fire be insured in this or any other company, this policy shall not extend to cover the same, excepting only as far as relates to any excess of value beyond the amount of such specific insurance, and shall not be liable for any loss unless the amount of such loss shall exceed the amount of such specific insurance (disregarding the liability of the assured as an insurer under any co-insurance clause, under such specific insurance), which said excess only is declared to be under the protection of this policy and subject to average aforesaid.

Other insurance permitted.

CONSEQUENTIAL DAMAGE CLAUSE.
Adopted January 11, 1906.

See also page 35.

This clause to be attached to all policies, other than those insuring brewery property, covering on Merchandise, Stocks or Products in houses artificially cooled, other than solely by the storage of ice.

Notice is hereby given, and it is understood and agreed, that the insurance under this policy does not extend in its application to cover, and this company shall not be liable for, any indirect or consequential loss or damage, including loss or damage caused by change of temperature resulting from, occasioned or caused by the total or partial destruction by fire of the refrigerating or cooling apparatus, connections or supply pipes, nor by the interruption of the refrigerating or cooling processes from any cause.

FORM NO. ONE, CONSEQUENTIAL DAMAGE FORM.—
(Single Source Equipment.)

Adopted January 11, 1906.

See also page 35.

The assuming of this liability by endorsement prohibited. *Specific policies covering only against consequential damages to be issued in all cases.*

This form to be used where but *one source of supply* for refrigeration is maintained. The charge under this form to be 50 per cent of the rate on the equipment in the building containing the refrigerating apparatus.

$........On Merchandise, Stocks, Products...............
....
....

The conditions of this Contract of Insurance are, That this Company agrees to be liable only for such loss or damage to the property covered, not exceeding the sum insured under this policy, as may be caused by change of temperature resulting from the total or partial destruction by fire of the refrigerating or cooling apparatus, connections or supply pipes, or by the interruption by fire of refrigerating or cooling processes.

It is understood and agreed that the liability assumed by this Company hereunder shall be only such proportion of the actual loss and damage above specified, as the amount insured under this policy bears to the total value of the property hereby covered.

FORM NO. TWO, CONSEQUENTIAL DAMAGE FORM.—
(Two-Source Equipment.)

Adopted January 11, 1906.

See also page 36.

The following form to be used in covering against consequential damage where *two sources of supply* for refrigeration (not exposed to each other) are maintained, the two-source supply having had the approval of the Superintendent of Ratings. *The assuming of this insurance by endorsement prohibited. Specific policies to be issued.*

The premium charged to be 25 per cent of the highest-rated equipment furnishing refrigeration referred to herein.

$........On Merchandise, Stocks, Products...............
....
....

The conditions of this Contract of Insurance are, That this Company agrees to be liable only for such loss or damage to the property covered, not exceeding the sum insured under this policy, as may be caused by change of temperature resulting from the total or partial destruction by fire of the refrigerating or cooling apparatus, connections or supply pipes, or by the interruption by fire of refrigerating or cooling processes.

It is understood and agreed that the liability assumed by this Company hereunder shall be only such proportion of the actual loss and damage above specified as the amount insured under this policy bears to the total value of the property hereby covered.

It is further understood and agreed, and made a warranty on the part of the assured, in consideration of the reduced rate of premium charged, that there shall be maintained at least two separate and complete plants for furnishing refrigeration, both being under the control of the owners or lessees of the building containing the property covered—to be kept in readiness at all times for instant use, and each of sufficient capacity to answer all demands should one refrigerating plant be damaged or destroyed.

CONTRACTOR'S FLOATER.

Rate 3 per cent. Advance applies.

Adopted January 11, 1906.

$........on his interest as contractor in buildings or other structures in process of erection or undergoing alterations or repairs, and on the furniture, fixtures, and other equipment thereof being installed therein, and on all materials, supplies, tools, implements and appliances used or for use in the construction and equipment thereof, his own or for which he is liable in the event of loss by fire, wherever located in the County of Cook, State of Illinois, except in or on the premises of the assured, in any storage warehouse, and except in any building occupied for wood working with power.

The interest of the assured, it is agreed, covers the value of all materials furnished by him that have entered into the structure, or are upon the premises, and of all work done thereon whether the work and/or materials have or have not been accepted.

In consideration of the rate at which this policy is written it is expressly stipulated and made a condition of this contract that this company shall be liable for no greater proportion of any loss than the amount hereby insured bears to the actual cash value of the property described herein at the time when such loss shall happen, nor for more than the proportion which this policy bears to the total contributing insurance thereon.

But it is at the same time declared and agreed that if the interest of the assured in any specific property described above, included in the terms of this policy, shall at the time of any fire be insured in this or any other company, this policy shall not extend to cover the same, excepting only as far as relates to any excess of value beyond the amount of such specific insurance, and shall not be liable for any loss unless the amount of such loss shall exceed the amount of such specific insurance (disregarding the liability of the assured

as an insurer under any co-insurance clause, under such specific insurance), which said excess only is declared to be under the protection of this policy and subject to average aforesaid.

Other insurance permitted.

CONTRIBUTION CLAUSE:

Adopted January 11, 1906.

In consideration of the rate at which this policy is written it is expressly stipulated and made a condition of this contract that this company shall be liable for no greater proportion of any loss than the amount hereby insured bears to .... per cent of the actual cash value of the property described herein at the time when such loss shall happen, nor for more than the proportion which this policy bears to the total contributing insurance thereon. If this policy be divided into two or more items, the foregoing conditions shall apply to each item separately.

ITEM CONTRIBUTION CLAUSE:

Adopted January 11, 1906.

In consideration of the rate at which this policy is written it is expressly stipulated and made a condition of this contract that this company shall be liable under........item of this policy for no greater proportion of any loss than the amount hereby insured bears to .... per cent of the actual cash value of the property described herein at the time when such loss shall happen, nor for more than the proportion which this policy bears to the total contributing insurance thereon.

CRUDE PETROLEUM PERMIT:

Adopted January 11, 1906.

See also page 37.

Permission may be granted for the use of crude petroleum or fuel oil for fuel, when the apparatus has been installed in accordance with the rules of The Chicago Board of Underwriters. Permits, when granted, must be under the following form:

In consideration of the warranties herein contained, permission is hereby granted for the use of crude petroleum or fuel oil for fuel.

Warranted by the assured that no change shall be made in the apparatus or the arrangement thereof, without the consent of this company in writing, and that no oil shall be used which does not stand a flash test of 150 deg. Fahr., the test to be made with a Tagliabue Cup.

ELECTRICAL APPARATUS FLOATER.

Rate, 3 per cent. Advance included.

Adopted **May 11, 1906**.

$........On dynamos, motors and other electrical apparatus, their own, or held by them in trust or on commission, or for which they may be legally liable, while contained in any building, except the premises of the assured, in Cook County, Illinois.

It is a part of the consideration for this policy and the basis upon which the rate of premium is fixed, that the assured shall maintain insurance upon the property described by this policy, to the extent of the actual cash value thereof, and that, failing so to do, the assured shall be an insurer to the extent of such deficit, and to that extent shall bear his, her or their proportion of any loss.

But it is at the same time declared and agreed that if any specific property described above, included in the terms of this policy, shall at the time of any fire be insured in this or any other company, this policy shall not extend to cover the same, excepting only as far as relates to any excess of value beyond the amount of such specific insurance, and shall not be liable for any loss unless the amount of such loss shall exceed the amount of such specific insurance (disregarding the liability of the assured as an insurer under any co-insurance clause, under such specific insurance), which said excess only is declared to be under the protection of this policy and subject to average aforesaid.

Other insurance permitted.

It is understood and agreed that this company shall not be liable for an amount exceeding 10 per cent of the amount of this policy for loss by any one fire.

ELECTRIC CURRENT CLAUSE.

Adopted January 11, 1906.

See also page 36.

It is understood and agreed that this insurance does not cover any loss or damage to electrical machinery, apparatus and connections in use caused by electric currents, whether artificial or natural.

ELECTRICAL EXEMPTION CLAUSE.

To be attached to all Policies covering Public or Private Electric Generating, Distributing, Transforming, or Storage Stations.

Adopted January 11, 1906.

See also page 33.

This company shall not be liable for any loss or damage resulting from any electrical injury or disturbance, whether from artificial or natural cause, in or to any of the electrical apparatus, machinery, or connections hereby insured unless fire ensues, and then for loss resulting from fire only.

ELECTROTYPE AND PRINTING SUPP

Adopted February 26th, 190'

Rate 2½ per cent., plus advan

$........On electrotypes, wood cuts, ste such other appurtenances and supplies, all whi building in Cook County, Illinois, except any and except the premises of the assured.

It is a part of the consideration for this p upon which the rate of premium is fixed, tha maintain insurance upon the property describe the extent of the actual cash value thereof, and the assured shall be an insurer to the extent of that extent shall bear his, her, or their proporti

But it is at the same time declared and interest of the assured in any specific proper included in the terms of this policy, shall, at tl be insured in this or any other company, this pol to cover the same, excepting only as far as rela value beyond the amount of such specific insur be liable for any loss, unless the amount of sucl the amount of such specific insurance (disregar the assured as an insurer under any co-insurance specific insurance) which said excess only is d the protection of this policy and subject to aver

Other insurance permitted.

This policy shall cover any direct loss or Lightning, except loss or damage to electri machinery and connections in use (meaning the accepted use of the term Lightning, and in no or damage by cyclone, tornado or windstorm), sum insured, nor the interest of the insured ir subject in all other respects to the terms and policy. *Provided*, however, if there shall be aı ance on said property, this company shall be l with such other insurance for any direct loss by such other insurance be against direct loss by I

ELECTRICAL APPARATUS FLOATER.

Rate, 3 per cent. Advance included.

Adopted May 11, 1906.

$........On dynamos, motors and other electrical apparatus, their own, or held by them in trust or on commission, or for which they may be legally liable, while contained in any building, except the premises of the assured, in Cook County, Illinois.

It is a part of the consideration for this policy and the basis upon which the rate of premium is fixed, that the assured shall maintain insurance upon the property described by this policy, to the extent of the actual cash value thereof, and that, failing so to do, the assured shall be an insurer to the extent of such deficit, and to that extent shall bear his, her or their proportion of any loss.

But it is at the same time declared and agreed that if any specific property described above, included in the terms of this policy, shall at the time of any fire be insured in this or any other company, this policy shall not extend to cover the same, excepting only as far as relates to any excess of value beyond the amount of such specific insurance, and shall not be liable for any loss unless the amount of such loss shall exceed the amount of such specific insurance (disregarding the liability of the assured as an insurer under any co-insurance clause, under such specific insurance), which said excess only is declared to be under the protection of this policy and subject to average aforesaid.

Other insurance permitted.

It is understood and agreed that this company shall not be liable for an amount exceeding 10 per cent of the amount of this policy for loss by any one fire.

ELECTRIC CURRENT CLAUSE.

Adopted January 11, 1906.

See also page 36.

It is understood and agreed that this insurance does not cover any loss or damage to electrical machinery, apparatus and connections in use caused by electric currents, whether artificial or natural.

ELECTRICAL EXEMPTION CLAUSE.

To be attached to all Policies covering Public or Private Electric Generating, Distributing, Transforming, or Storage Stations.

Adopted January 11, 1906.

See also page 33.

This company shall not be liable for any loss or damage resulting from any electrical injury or disturbance, whether from artificial or natural cause, in or to any of the electrical apparatus, machinery, or connections hereby insured unless fire ensues, and then for loss resulting from fire only.

ELECTROTYPE AND PRINTING SUPPLIES FLOATER.
Adopted February 26th, 1907.
Rate 2½ per cent., plus advance.

$.........On electrotypes, wood cuts, stereotypes, type and such other appurtenances and supplies, all while contained in any building in Cook County, Illinois, except any storage warehouse and except the premises of the assured.

It is a part of the consideration for this policy and the basis upon which the rate of premium is fixed, that the assured shall maintain insurance upon the property described by this policy, to the extent of the actual cash value thereof, and that failing so to do the assured shall be an insurer to the extent of such deficit, and to that extent shall bear his, her, or their proportion of any loss.

But it is at the same time declared and agreed, that if the interest of the assured in any specific property described above, included in the terms of this policy, shall, at the time of any fire, be insured in this or any other company, this policy shall not extend to cover the same, excepting only as far as relates to any excess of value beyond the amount of such specific insurance, and shall not be liable for any loss, unless the amount of such loss shall exceed the amount of such specific insurance (disregarding the liability of the assured as an insurer under any co-insurance clause, under such specific insurance) which said excess only is declared to be under the protection of this policy and subject to average aforesaid.

Other insurance permitted.

This policy shall cover any direct loss or damage caused by Lightning, except loss or damage to electrical apparatus and machinery and connections in use (meaning thereby the commonly accepted use of the term Lightning, and in no case to include loss or damage by cyclone, tornado or windstorm), not exceeding the sum insured, nor the interest of the insured in the property, and subject in all other respects to the terms and conditions of this policy. *Provided*, however, if there shall be any other fire insurance on said property, this company shall be liable only pro rata with such other insurance for any direct loss by Lightning, whether such other insurance be against direct loss by Lightning or not.

GASOLINE ENGINE PERMIT.

Adopted January 11, 1906.

See also page 31.

In consideration of the compliance by the assured with the hereinafter named warranty, permission is hereby granted for the use of .... Gasoline Engine in the building described in this policy.

Warranted by the assured that the supply tank for gasoline shall not exceed in capacity two barrels, that it shall be located outside the building underground below the level of the lowest pipe in the building, that the gasoline shall be drawn through iron piping to the engine by a pump, that the piping and apparatus shall be so arranged that in case of accident to the same the gasoline will drain back to the tank, that the gasoline reservoir at the engine shall not exceed in capacity one gallon, and shall be provided with an overflow so as to drain through iron piping back to the tank, and that the engine when set on wood floor shall have placed beneath it a metal plate turned up at the edges.

PERMIT FOR THE USE OF GASOLINE FOR LIGHTING IN AIR PRESSURE LAMPS.

(This permit must not be issued for gravity pressure lamps.)

Adopted January 11, 1906.

See also page 31.

In consideration of the assured's compliance with the hereinafter named warranties, permission is hereby granted to use the vapor of gasoline for lighting purposes in the premises described in this policy, when not in violation of the law, the apparatus and device for generation and use of same being an air pressure lamp known as the.............manufactured by ....at....................

Warranted by the assured that no artificial light be permitted in the room when the reservoir is being filled; that the reservoir shall be located below the burner and shall not exceed two quarts capacity of gasoline; and that at no time shall there be to exceed one gallon of naphtha, gasoline or benzine for each occupant (except that in the lamp reservoir, which shall not exceed one quart) within said building or additions, and that kept in approved metal safety can, free from leak, and away from artificial light or heat. The lamp reservoir to be filled by daylight only, and not in the same room or room adjoining (having open communication) where or while any fire, blaze or artificial light or flame of any kind is burning.

CAUTION.—The principal danger from gasoline lamps is in having the gasoline about. At ordinary temperature gasoline continually gives off inflammable and explosive vapor, and a flame some distance from the material will ignite it through the medium of this vapor. It is said that one pint of gasoline will

impregnate 200 cubic feet of air and make it explosive; and it depends upon the proportion of air and vapor whether it becomes a burning gas or destructive explosive. Beware of any leaks and never forget how dangerous a material you are using.

PERMIT FOR USE OF GASOLINE FOR LIGHTING.
(In gravity lamps only.)

Adopted January 11, 1906.

See also page 31.

In consideration of the assured's compliance with the hereinafter named warranties permission is hereby given to use the vapor of gasoline for lighting purposes in the premises described in this policy when not in violation of the law, the apparatus and device for generation and use of same being a gravity lamp and known as the .... manufactured by ....at...................

Warranted by the assured that no artificial light be permitted in the room when the reservoir is being filled; that the reservoir shall not exceed one quart capacity; that at no time shall there be to exceed one gallon of naphtha, gasoline or benzine for each occupant (except that in the lamp reservoir, which shall not exceed one quart) within said building or additions, and that kept in an approved metal safety can, free from leak, and away from artificial light or heat. The lamp reservoir to be filled and the gasoline (or fluid under whatever name) handled by daylight only, and not in the same room or room adjoining (having open communication) where or while any fire, blaze or artificial light or flame of any kind is burning.

CAUTION—.The danger in gasoline lamps is not so much in themselves as in having the material about. At ordinary temperature gasoline continually gives off inflammable vapor, and a light some distance from the material will ignite it through the medium of this vapor. It is said that one pint of gasoline will impregnate 200 cubic feet of air and make it explosive; and it depends upon the proportion of air or vapor whether it becomes a burning gas or destructive explosive. Beware of any leaks in cans, and never forget how dangerous a material you are handling.

PERMIT FOR USE OF GASOLINE FOR LIGHTING.
(Oil Distribution Systems.)

Adopted January 11, 1906.

See also page 31.

In consideration of $........ additional premium and the assured's compliance with the hereinafter named warranties, permission is hereby given, where not in violation of any law, statute or municipal restriction, to light the premises described

in this policy from a .... gasoline oil distribution system manufactured by......................at......................

It is warranted by the assured that the reservoirs and tanks used in connection with this system shall be located outside the building at least five feet removed therefrom below the level of the lowest pipe in the building used in connection with the apparatus; that they shall be so arranged that under normal conditions the only gasoline in the building will be that contained in the pipe system, and so that under no possible condition can more than one gallon of gasoline be accidentally admitted at one time within the building; that they shall be filled by daylight only, and that no blaze or artificial light shall be allowed in their vicinity.

The term gasoline shall be held to include naphtha, benzine or any of the light products of petroleum by whatever name known.

CAUTION.—The principal danger from gasoline lamps is in having the gasoline about. At ordinary temperature gasoline continually gives off inflammable and explosive vapor, and a flame some distance from the material will ignite it through the medium of this vapor. It is said that one pint of gasoline will impregnate 200 cubic feet of air and make it explosive; and it depends upon the proportion of air and vapor whether it becomes a burning gas or destructive explosive. Beware of any leaks, and never forget how dangerous a material you are using.

GASOLINE STOVE PERMIT

Adopted January 11, 1906.

See also page 31.

Permission is hereby given for the use of.......... gasoline or vapor stove.......... in the building described in this policy, but only under the following restrictions and conditions, to be observed by the assured, viz.: that at no time shall there be to exceed one gallon of naphtha, gasoline or benzine for each occupant (except that in the stove reservoir, which shall not exceed one gallon) within said building or additions, and that kept in an approved metal safety can, free from leak, and away from artificial light or heat. The stove reservoir to be filled and the gasoline (or fluid under whatever name) handled by daylight only, and not in the same room or room adjoining (having open communication) where or while any fire, blaze or artificial light or flame of any kind is burning.

NOTE.—The danger from gasoline stoves is not so much in the stoves themselves as in the material used in them. At ordinary temperature gasoline continually gives off inflammable vapor, and light some distance from the material will ignite it through the medium of this vapor. It is said that one pint of gasoline will impregnate 200 cubic feet of air and make it explosive; and it depends upon the proportions of air or vapor whether it becomes a burning gas or destructive explosive. As gasoline vapor is

heavier than air, its tendency is to settle, therefore should not be stored in cellars or low places. Beware of any leaks in cans, and never forget how dangerous a material you are handling.

HASTINGS EXPRESS CO.—Floater.

Adopted January 11, 1906.

Rate under this form, 75 cents. Advance applies.

$........On goods, wares, merchandise, baggage and other personal property, its own or held by it in trust, or as common carriers, while contained in cars on railway tracks in Cook County, Illinois, except all tracks within buildings, and all tracks located within the district bounded by 39th Street, 47th Street, Halsted Street and Ashland Avenue, in the City of Chicago, and on advanced and earned charges on the property of others.

This policy does not attach to or cover on any property otherwise or elsewhere insured.

Claim for loss to property of others held by the assured is hereby limited to the amount paid by assured for such loss to owner, consignor or consignee, which shall not exceed the cash value of the property destroyed nor the actual loss sustained.

Claim for loss is hereby limited to not exceeding twenty-four hundred dollars on contents of any one car, and it is hereby agreed that in the event of partial loss to contents of any one car, and the value of the contents of such car exceeds twenty-four hundred dollars, then this Company shall be liable for such proportion of the loss and damage as said limited amount shall bear to the value of the contents of said car. Beyond the exercise of due diligence the assured shall not be held accountable for loss arising from the handling and transportation of articles prohibited under this policy.

It is agreed that the assured shall at all times during the term hereof maintain insurance on the property described to the amount of ten thousand dollars, be an insurer to the extent of any deficit therein and as such bear its portion of any loss.

It is understood and agreed that in case this policy is reduced by loss payments, that it shall be reinstated to the original amount for the remainder of its term at pro. rata of the premium originally charged for the remainder of the term.

Whenever this Company shall pay the assured any claim for loss under this policy and shall claim that any person or corporation other than the assured is liable therefor, whether caused by the act or neglect of such person or corporation or otherwise, this Company shall at once be legally subrogated to all the rights of the assured to the extent of such payment, and such rights shall be duly assigned to this Company at the time of such payment.

Permission is granted to load and unload said cars when on tracks within the County of Cook, covered hereunder at all hours, and to use artificial light.

This policy shall cover any direct loss or damage caused by lightning (meaning thereby the commonly accepted use of the term lightning, and in no case to include loss or damage by cyclone, tornado or wind storm), not exceeding the sum insured, nor the interest of the insured in the property, and subject in all other respects to the terms and conditions of this policy. *Provided*, however, if there shall be any other fire insurance on said property, this Company shall be liable only pro rata with such other insurance for any direct loss by lightning, whether such other insurance be against direct loss by lightning or not.

HASTINGS EXPRESS CO.—Car Floater.

Adopted January 11, 1906.

Rate under this form, 75 cents. Advance applies.

$........ being $........ on each of freight cars numbered .... while on tracks and in yards in Cook County, Illinois, except that district within the City of Chicago bounded by 39th Street, 47th Street and S. Halsted Street and Ashland Avenue, *excluding tracks in buildings.* Beyond the exercise of due diligence the assured shall not be held accountable for loss arising from the handling and transportation of articles prohibited under this policy.

Permission is granted to load and unload said cars within the County of Cook at all hours. To use artificial light without prejudice to this policy.

Whenever this Company shall pay the assured any claim for loss under this policy and shall claim that any person or corporation other than the assured is liable therefor, whether caused by the act or neglect of such person or corporation, or otherwise, this Company shall at once be legally subrogated to all rights of the assured to the extent of such payment, and such rights shall be duly assigned to this Company at the time of such payment.

This policy shall cover any direct loss or damage caused by lightning (meaning thereby the commonly accepted use of the term lightning, and in no case to include loss or damage by cyclone, tornado or wind storm), not exceeding the sum insured, nor the interest of the insured in the property and subject in all other respects to the terms and conditions of this policy. *Provided*, however, if there shall be any other fire insurance on said property, this Company shall be liable only pro rata with such other insurance for any direct loss by lightning, whether such other insurance be against direct loss by lightning or not.

In consideration of the rate at which this policy is written it is expressly stipulated and made a condition of this contract that this company shall be liable for no greater proportion of any loss than the amount hereby insured bears to eighty per cent of the actual cash value of the property described herein at the time

This policy shall cover any direct loss or damage caused by lightning (meaning thereby the commonly accepted use of the term lightning, and in no case to include loss or damage by cyclone, tornado or wind storm), not exceeding the sum insured, nor the interest of the insured in the property, and subject in all other respects to the terms and conditions of this policy. *Provided*, however, if there shall be any other fire insurance on said property, this Company shall be liable only pro rata with such other insurance for any direct loss by lightning, whether such other insurance be against direct loss by lightning or not.

HASTINGS EXPRESS CO.—Car Floater.

Adopted January 11, 1906.

Rate under this form, 75 cents. Advance applies.

$........ being $........ on each of freight cars numbered .... while on tracks and in yards in Cook County, Illinois, except that district within the City of Chicago bounded by 39th Street, 47th Street and S. Halsted Street and Ashland Avenue, *excluding tracks in buildings*. Beyond the exercise of due diligence the assured shall not be held accountable for loss arising from the handling and transportation of articles prohibited under this policy.

Permission is granted to load and unload said cars within the County of Cook at all hours. To use artificial light without prejudice to this policy.

Whenever this Company shall pay the assured any claim for loss under this policy and shall claim that any person or corporation other than the assured is liable therefor, whether caused by the act or neglect of such person or corporation, or otherwise, this Company shall at once be legally subrogated to all rights of the assured to the extent of such payment, and such rights shall be duly assigned to this Company at the time of such payment.

This policy shall cover any direct loss or damage caused by lightning (meaning thereby the commonly accepted use of the term lightning, and in no case to include loss or damage by cyclone, tornado or wind storm), not exceeding the sum insured, nor the interest of the insured in the property and subject in all other respects to the terms and conditions of this policy. *Provided*, however, if there shall be any other fire insurance on said property, this Company shall be liable only pro rata with such other insurance for any direct loss by lightning, whether such other insurance be against direct loss by lightning or not.

In consideration of the rate at which this policy is written it is expressly stipulated and made a condition of this contract that this company shall be liable for no greater proportion of any loss than the amount hereby insured bears to eighty per cent of the actual cash value of the property described herein at the time

when such loss shall happen, nor for more than the proportion which this policy bears to the total contributing insurance thereon. If this policy be divided into two or more items, the foregoing conditions shall apply to each item separately.

HASTINGS EXPRESS CO. FLOATER.—Covering Cars in Repair Shops.

Adopted January 11, 1906.

Rate under this form 3 per cent. Advance applies.

$300.00. On any one of the eight cars of assured while in repair or otherwise in any repair shop in Cook County, except within the district bounded by 39th, 47th and Halsted streets and Ashland avenue.

It is understood and agreed that whenever this company shall pay the assured any sum for loss under this policy, and shall claim that any person or corporation other than the assured is liable therefor, whether caused by the act or neglect of such person or corporation, or otherwise, this company shall at once be legally subrogated to all the rights of assured to the extent of such payments, and such rights shall be duly assigned to this company at the time such payments are made.

This policy shall cover any direct loss or damage caused by lightning (meaning thereby the commonly accepted use of the term lightning, and in no case to include loss or damage by cyclone, tornado or wind storm), not exceeding the sum insured, nor the interest of the insured in the property and subject in all other respects to the terms and conditions of this policy, *Provided*, however, if there shall be any other fire insurance on said property, this Company shall be liable only pro rata with such other insurance for any direct loss by lightning, whether such other insurance be against direct loss by lightning or not.

In consideration of the rate at which this policy is written it is expressly stipulated and made a condition of this contract that this company shall be liable for no greater proportion of any loss than the amount hereby insured bears to eighty per cent of the actual cash value of the property described herein at the time when such loss shall happen, nor for more than the proportion which this policy bears to the total contributing insurance thereon. If this policy be divided into two or more items, the foregoing conditions shall apply to each item separately.

HOUSE FURNISHINGS AND DECORATIONS FLOATER IN PRIVATE RESIDENCES.

Adopted January 11, 1906.

Rate, 1 per cent. Advance applies.

$........On merchandise, the property of the assured, or for which they may be legally liable, consisting chiefly of house furnishings and decorations, while contained in any building

HOUSE FURNISHINGS AND DECORATIONS FLOATER IN PRIVATE RESIDENCES.

Adopted January 11, 1906. Amended February 26, 1907.

Rate 1 per cent. Advance applies.

$........On merchandise, tools, implements and materials, the property of the assured, or for which they may be legally liable, consisting chiefly of house furnishings and decorations, while contained in any building occupied or to be occupied exclusively for private residence purposes, and not elsewhere, and situate in the County of Cook, State of Illinois. (Form otherwise unchanged).

occupied or to be occupied exclusively for private residence purposes, and not elsewhere, and situate in the County of Cook, State of Illinois.

It is understood and agreed that this policy covers the interest of the assured in improvements made by the assured to such buildings, and it is also understood and agreed that this policy covers merchandise, the property of the assured, or for which they are legally liable, while contained in any building as above described, and improvements of all kinds added to such buildings by the assured while such buildings are being furnished, decorated or improved in whole or in part by the assured under contract, the liability under this policy ceasing and terminating on the acceptance of such merchandise or improvements by the party or parties with whom the contract is made.

Privilege granted for mechanics to make alterations and repairs to the buildings above described, and for such buildings to be unoccupied.

In consideration of the rate at which this policy is written it is expressly stipulated and made a condition of this contract that this company shall be liable for no greater proportion of any loss than the amount hereby insured bears to the actual cash value of the property described herein at the time when such loss shall happen, nor for more than the proportion which this policy bears to the total contributing insurance thereon.

But it is at the same time declared and agreed that if any specific property described above, included in the terms of this policy, shall at the time of any fire be insured in this or any other company, this policy shall not extend to cover the same, excepting only as far as relates to any excess of value beyond the amount of such specific insurance, and shall not be liable for any loss unless the amount of such loss shall exceed the amount of such specific insurance (disregarding the liability of the assured as an insurer under any co-insurance clause, under such specific insurance), which said excess only is declared to be under the protection of this policy and subject to average aforesaid.

Other insurance permitted.

It is understood and agreed that this Company shall not be liable for an amount exceeding 20 per cent of the amount of this policy for loss by any one fire.

This policy shall cover any direct loss or damage caused by lightning (meaning thereby the commonly accepted use of the term lightning, and in no case to include loss or damage by cyclone, tornado or wind storm), not exceeding the sum insured, nor the interest of the insured in the property and subject in all other respects to the terms and conditions of this policy. *Provided*, however, if there shall be any other fire insurance on said property, this Company shall be liable only pro rata with such other insurance for any direct loss by lightning, whether such other insurance be against direct loss by lightning or not.

Permission is hereby given for the use of .... Gasoline or Vapor Stove..........in the building described in this policy, but only under the following restrictions and conditions,

to be observed by the assured, viz., that at no time shall there be to exceed one gallon of naphtha, gasoline or benzine for each occupant (except that in the stove reservoir within said building or additions), and that kept in an approved metal safety can free from leak and away from artificial light or heat. The stove reservoir to be filled and the gasoline (or fluid under whatever name) handled by daylight only, and not in the same room or room adjoining (having open communication) where or while any fire, blaze or artificial light or flame of any kind is burning.

NOTE.—The danger from gasoline stoves is not so much from the stoves themselves as in the material used in them. At ordinary temperature gasoline continually gives off inflammable vapor, and light some distance from the material will ignite it through the medium of this vapor. It is said that one pint of gasoline will impregnate 200 cubic feet of air and make it explosive; and it depends upon the proportions of air and vapor whether it becomes a burning gas or a destructive explosive. As gasoline vapor is heavier than air its tendency is to settle, therefore should not be stored in cellars or low places. Beware of leaks in cans, and never forget how dangerous a material you are handling.

HOUSEHOLD FURNITURE FLOATER.

Adopted January 11, 1906.

Rate, 3 per cent. Advance applies.

$........On household furniture and household goods, their own or in which they may have an interest, or for which they may be liable, while contained in any building except a storage warehouse and except the premises of the assured in Cook County, Illinois.

In consideration of the rate at which this policy is written it is expressly stipulated and made a condition of this contract that this company shall be liable for no greater proportion of any loss than the amount hereby insured bears to the actual cash value of the property described herein at the time when such loss shall happen, nor for more than the proportion which this policy bears to the total contributing insurance thereon.

But it is at the same time declared and agreed that if any specific property described above, included in the terms of this policy, shall at the time of any fire be insured in this or any other company, this policy shall not extend to cover the same, excepting only as far as relates to any excess of value beyond the amount of such specific insurance, and shall not be liable for any loss unless the amount of such loss shall exceed the amount of such specific insurance (disregarding the liability of the assured as an insurer under any co-insurance clause, under such specific insurance), which said excess only is declared to be under the protection of this policy and subject to average aforesaid.

Other insurance permitted.

It is understood and agreed that this Company shall not be liable for an amount exceeding twenty per cent of the amount of this policy for loss by any one fire.

LIGHTNING CLAUSE NO. ONE.

Adopted January 11, 1906.

See also page 36.

To be used on policies *Insuring Electrical Apparatus* alone or with other subjects.

This policy shall cover any direct loss or damage caused by lightning, except loss or damage to electrical apparatus and machinery and connections in use (meaning thereby the commonly accepted use of the term lightning, and in no case to include loss or damage by cyclone, tornado or windstorm), not exceeding the sum insured, nor the interest of the insured in the property, and subject in all other respects to the terms and conditions of this policy. *Provided*, however, if there shall be any other fire insurance on said property this Company shall be liable only pro rata with such other insurance for any direct loss by lightning, whether such other insurance be against direct loss by lightning or not.

LIGHTNING CLAUSE NO. TWO.

Adopted January 11, 1906.

To be used only on policies where *Electrical Apparatus is not* one of the subjects of insurance.

This policy shall cover any direct loss or damage caused by lightning (meaning thereby the commonly accepted use of the term lightning, and in no case to include loss or damage by cyclone, tornado or wind storm) not exceeding the sum insured, nor the interest of the insured in the property, and subject in all other respects to the terms and conditions of this policy. *Provided*, however, if there shall be any other fire insurance on said property this company shall be liable only pro rata with such other insurance for any direct loss by lightning, whether such other insurance be against direct loss by lightning or not.

LIMITED LOSS CLAIM FORM—BUILDINGS FIRE PROOF CONSTRUCTION.

Adopted January 11, 1906.

"In consideration of the rate at which this policy is written, it is expressly stipulated and made a condition of this contract that no claim shall be made for loss unless the whole loss to the property by any one fire shall exceed the sum of............ Dollars, and in that event this company shall be liable for no greater proportion of the excess of any loss over and above said sum of .... Dollars than the amount hereby in-

sured bears to .. per cent of the actual cash value of the property described herein at the time when such loss shall happen, nor for more than the proportion which this policy bears to the total contributing insurance thereon. It is further expressly stipulated and made a condition of this policy that the assured shall retain at his own risk and uninsured the .... Dollars above excluded, or this policy shall be void."

LINCOLN WAREHOUSE AND VAN CO. FLOATER.

Adopted January 11, 1906.

Rate under this form, 1 per cent. Advance applies.

$........On Goods—Vans, only while located outside any building in Cook County, Illinois.

It is hereby declared and agreed that in case the property aforesaid in all the places or limits, included in this insurance, shall, at the breaking out of any fire or fires, be collectively of greater value than the sum insured, then this company shall pay and make good such portion only of the loss or damage as the sum hereby insured shall bear to the whole value of the property aforesaid, at the time when such fire or fires shall first happen.

But it is at the same time declared and agreed that if any specific van included in the terms of this policy, or such van in any specified place or places, within the limits of this insurance, shall at the time of any fire be insured in this or any other company, this policy shall not extend to cover the same, excepting only as far as relates to any excess of value beyond the amount of such specific insurance or insurances, and shall not be liable for any loss unless the amount of such loss shall exceed the amount of such specific insurance or insurances, which said excess only is declared to be under the protection of this policy and subject to average aforesaid.

It being the true intent and meaning of this agreement that this company shall not be liable for any loss, unless the amount of such loss shall exceed the amount of the specific insurance or insurances, and then only for such excess, which said excess shall be subject to average as above.

Other insurance permitted without notice until required.

LOSS PAYABLE CLAUSE.

Adopted January 11, 1906.

Loss Payable Clause. To be used in all cases where policies or certificates are made payable to assured or order hereon.

See also pages 38 and 44.

Loss, if any, payable to assured or order hereon; but this insurance is void as to any subsequent owner or purchaser of the property hereby insured. It is understood, however, that this insurance shall not become void on account of any pledge of the property as collateral.

LUMBER EXCLUSION CLAUSE.

Adopted January 11, 1906.

To be attached to all Policies covering on property in Lumber Yards at Lumber Yard Rate.

It is understood that insurance under this policy does not cover on or in any building used for Woodworking, Dry Kilns or Manufacturing purposes.

FORM OF LUMBER VACANCY CLAUSE.

Adopted January 11, 1906.

See also page 42.

Warranted by the assured that the streets adjoining the above described premises shall be kept clear of lumber and other materials, and that a clear space of .... feet shall at all times be maintained between the above described premises and ....
....
or this policy shall be void.

However, this shall not be construed to prohibit the loading and unloading within or transportation of lumber and timber products across such streets, alleys and clear space.

MEAT MARKET (RETAIL) FLOATER.

Adopted January 11, 1906.

Rate under this form, 3 per cent. Advance applies.

$........On their interest in furniture, fixtures and tools, while contained in any retail meat market in the United States.

In consideration of the rate at which this policy is written it is expressly stipulated and made a condition of this contract that this company shall be liable for no greater proportion of any loss than the amount hereby insured bears to the actual cash value of the property described herein at the time when such loss shall happen, nor for more than the proportion which this policy bears to the total contributing insurance thereon.

But it is at the same time declared and agreed that if any specific property described above, included in the terms of this policy, shall at the time of any fire be insured in this or any other company, this policy shall not extend to cover the same, excepting only as far as relates to any excess of value beyond the amount of such specific insurance, and shall not be liable for any loss unless the amount of such loss shall exceed the amount of such specific insurance (disregarding the liability of the assured as an insurer under any co-insurance clause, under such specific insurance), which said excess only is declared to be under the protection of this policy and subject to average aforesaid.

Other insurance permitted.

It is understood and agreed that this company shall not be liable for an amount exceeding its proportion of one thousand dollars ($1,000) for loss by any one fire.

FLOATER FORM FOR MERCHANDISE IN CARS ON TRACK.

Adopted January 11, 1906.

Rate under this form, 1 per cent. Advance applies.

$........On merchandise, their own, or held by them in trust or on commission or on consignment, or sold but not delivered, or for which they may be legally liable, while contained in cars on railway tracks in Cook County, Illinois, except all tracks located inside buildings and all tracks located in the territory bounded by 39th street, Halsted street, 47th street and Ashland avenue, in the City of Chicago, Illinois.

In consideration of the rate at which this policy is written it is expressly stipulated and made a condition of this contract that this company shall be liable for no greater proportion of any loss than the amount hereby insured bears to the actual cash value of the property described herein at the time when such loss shall happen, nor for more than the proportion which this policy bears to the total contributing insurance thereon.

But it is at the same time declared and agreed that if any specific parcel of goods included in the terms of this policy, in any place or places within the limits of this insurance shall at the time of any fire be insured in this or any other company, this policy shall not extend to cover the same, excepting only as far as relates to any excess of value beyond the amount of such specific insurance, and shall not be liable for any loss unless the amount of such loss shall exceed the amount of such specific insurance (disregarding the liability of the assured as an insurer under any co-insurance clause, under such specific insurance), which said excess only is declared to be under the protection of this policy and subject to average aforesaid. If this company shall claim that any person or corporation, private or municipal, is responsible for the loss, whether caused by the act or neglect by such person or corporation, or otherwise, this company shall, on the payment of the loss, be subrogated to the extent of such payment to all right of recovery by the insured for the loss, and such right shall be assigned to this company by the insured on receiving such payment.

Other insurance permitted.

FLOATER FORM FOR MERCHANDISE IN CARS ON TRACK IN UNION STOCK YARDS.

Adopted January 11, 1906.

Rate under this form 1½ per cent. Advance applies.

$........On Merchandise, consisting chiefly of live stock and products of same, their own, or held by them in trust or on commission, or sold but not delivered, all while contained in cars wherever located in the district bounded on the north by 39th Street and the Union Stock Yards slip, on the east by Halsted Street, on the south by 47th Street, and on the west by Ashland Avenue, Chicago, Illinois.

Other insurance permitted.

It is understood and agreed that this insurance does not apply while said cars are in any building.

Loss, if any, payable to assured or order hereon, but this insurance is void as to any subsequent owner or purchaser of the property hereby insured. It is understood, however, that this insurance shall not become void on account of any pledge of the property as collateral.

In consideration of the rate at which this policy is written it is expressly stipulated and made a condition of this contract that this company shall be liable for no greater proportion of any loss than the amount hereby insured bears to 80 per cent of the actual cash value of the property described herein at the time when such loss shall happen, nor for more than the proportion which this policy bears to the total contributing insurance thereon.

It is hereby declared and agreed that if this company shall claim that any person or corporation, private or municipal, is responsible for the loss, whether caused by the act or neglect by such person or corporation, or otherwise, this company shall, on the payment of the loss, be subrogated to the extent of such payment to all right of recovery by the insured for the loss, and such right shall be assigned to this company by the insured on receiving such payment.

GENERAL MERCHANDISE FLOATER.

Adopted January 11, 1906.

Rate 3 per cent. Advance applies.

$........On merchandise, manufactured and in process of manufacture, and materials therefor, their own, or held by them in trust or on commission, or sold but not removed, or for which they may be legally liable, including goods left on storage, or for repairs, while contained in any building except storage warehouses, and except the premises of the assured in Cook county, Illinois.

In consideration of the rate at which this policy is written it is expressly stipulated and made a condition of this contract that this company shall be liable for no greater proportion of any loss than the amount hereby insured bears to the actual cash value of the property described herein at the time when such loss shall happen, nor for more than the proportion which this policy bears to the total contributing insurance thereon.

But it is at the same time declared and agreed, that if any specific property described above, included in the terms of this policy, shall at the time of any fire be insured in this or any other company, this policy shall not extend to cover the same, excepting only as far as relates to any excess of value beyond the amount of such specific insurance, and shall not be liable for any loss unless the amount of such loss shall exceed the amount of such specific insurance (disregarding the liability of the assured as an insurer under any co-insurance clause,

under such specific insurance), which said excess only is declared to be under the protection of this policy and subject to average aforesaid.

Other insurance permitted.

It is understood and agreed that this company shall not be liable for an amount exceeding ten per cent of the amount of this policy for loss by any one fire.

MACHINERY, WOOD AND METAL WORKING FLOATER.

Adopted April 6, 1906.

Rate under this form 4 per cent. Advance applies.

$........On wood and metal working machinery, their own or in which they may have an interest, or for which they may be liable while contained in any building in Cook County, except general storage warehouses, and the premises of the assured.

In consideration of the rate at which this policy is written it is expressly stipulated and made a condition of this contract that this company shall be liable for no greater proportion of any loss than the amount hereby insured bears to the actual cash value of the property described herein at the time when such loss shall happen, nor for more than the proportion which this policy bears to the total contributing insurance thereon.

But it is at the same time declared and agreed, that if any specific property described above, included in the terms of this policy, shall, at the time of any fire, be insured in this or any other company, this policy shall not extend to cover the same, excepting only as far as relates to any excess of value beyond the amount of such specific insurance, and shall not be liable for any loss unless the amount of such loss shall exceed the amount of such specific insurance (disregarding the liability of the assured as an insurer under any co-insurance clause, under such specific insurance) which said excess only is declared to be under the protection of this policy and subject to average aforesaid.

Other insurance permitted.

It is understood and agreed that. this company shall not be liable for an amount exceeding 10 per cent of the amount of this policy for loss by any one fire.

MORTGAGE CLAUSE. WITHOUT CONTRIBUTION.

Adopted January 11, 1906.

Loss or damage, if any, under this Policy shall be payable to ....mortagee [or trustee] or successor in trust, as interest may appear, and this insurance, as to the interest of the mortgagee [or trustee] only therein, shall not be invalidated by any act or neglect of the mortgagor or the owner of the within

described property, nor by any foreclosure or other proceedings or notice of sale relating to the property, nor by any change in the title or ownership of the property, nor by the occupation of the premises for purposes more hazardous than are permitted by this Policy: *Provided*, that in case the mortgagor or owner shall neglect to pay any premium due under this Policy, the mortgagee [or trustee] shall, on demand, pay the same.

PROVIDED also, that the mortgagee [or trustee] shall notify this Company of any change of ownership or occupancy or increase of hazard which shall come to the knowledge of said mortgagee [or trustee], and, unless permitted, by this Policy, it shall be noted thereon and the mortgagee [or trustee] shall, on demand, pay the premium of such increased hazard for the term of the use thereof, otherwise this Policy shall be null and void.

This company reserves the right to cancel this Policy at any time as provided by its terms, but in such case this Policy shall continue in force for the benefit only of the mortgagee [or trustee] for ten days after notice to the mortgagee [or trustee] of such cancellation and shall then cease, and this Company shall have the right, on like notice, to cancel this agreement.

Whenever this Company shall pay the mortgagee [or trustee] any sum for loss or damage under this Policy and shall claim that, as to the mortgagor or owner, no liability therefor existed, this Company shall, to the extent of such payment, be thereupon legally subrogated to all the rights of the party to whom such payment shall be made, under all securities held as collateral to the mortgage debt, or may, at its option, pay to the mortgagee [or trustee] the whole principal due or to grow due on the mortgage with interest, and shall thereupon receive a full assignment and transfer of the mortgage and of all such other securities; but no subrogation shall impair the right of the mortgagee [or trustee] to recover the full amount of .... claim.

MORTGAGE CLAUSE WITH FULL CONTRIBUTION.

Adopted January 11, 1906.

Loss or damage, if any, under this Policy shall be payable to ....as..............mortgagee [or trustee], as interest may appear, and this insurance, as to the interest of the mortgagee [or trustee] only therein, shall not be invalidated by any act or neglect of the mortgagor or the owner of the within described property, nor by any foreclosure or other proceedings or notice of sale relating to the property, nor by any change in the title or ownership of the property, nor by the occupation of the premises for purposes more hazardous than are permitted in this Policy: *Provided*, that in case the mortgagor or owner shall neglect to pay any premium due under this Policy, the mortgagee [or trustee] shall, on demand, pay the same.

PROVIDED also, that the mortgagee [or trustee] shall notify this Company of any change of ownership or occupancy or in-

crease of hazard which shall come to the knowledge of said mortgagee [or trustee], and, unless permitted by this Policy, it shall be noted thereon and the mortgagee [or trustee] shall, on demand, pay the premium for such increased hazard for the term of the use thereof, otherwise this Policy shall be null and void.

This Company reserves the right to cancel this Policy at any time as provided by its terms, but in such case this Policy shall continue in force for the benefit only of the mortgagee [or trustee] for ten days after notice to the mortgagee [or trustee] of such cancellation and shall then cease, and this Company shall have the right, on like notice, to cancel this agreement.

In case of any other insurance upon the within described property, this Company shall not be liable under this Policy for a greater proportion of any loss or damage sustained than the sum hereby insured bears to the whole amount of insurance on said property, issued to or held by any party or parties having an insurable interest therein, whether as owner, mortgagee or otherwise.

Whenever this Company shall pay the mortgagee [or trustee] any sum, for loss or damage under this Policy and shall claim that, as to the mortgagor or owner, no liability therefor existed, this Company shall, to the extent of such payment, be thereupon legally subrogated to all the rights of the party to whom such payment shall be made, under all securities held as collateral to the mortgage debt, or may, at its option, pay to the mortgagee [or trustee] the whole principal due or to grow due on the mortgage with interest, and shall thereupon receive a full assignment and transfer of the mortgage and of all such other securities, but no subrogation shall impair the right of the of the mortgagee [or trustee] to recover the full amount ot .... claim.

MUTOSCOPE COMPANY FLOATER.

Adopted January 11, 1906.

Rate under this form, 2½ per cent. Advance applies.

$........All while contained in any building in Cook County, Illinois, excluding their own premises and all warehouses occupied for storage of furntiure and fixtures and all manufacturing plants of any kind or nature.

In consideration of the rate at which this policy is written it is expressly stipulated and made a condition of this contract that this company shall be liable for no greater proportion of any loss than the amount hereby insured bears to the actual cash value of the property described herein at the time when such loss shall happen, nor for more than the proportion which this policy bears to the total contributing insurance thereon.

But it is at the same time declared and agreed that if any specific property described above, included in the terms of this policy, shall at the time of any fire be insured in this or any other i

company, this policy shall not extend to cover the same, excepting only as far as relates to any excess of value beyond the amount of such specific insurance, and shall not be liable for any loss unless the amount of such loss shall exceed the amount of such specific insurance (disregarding the liability of the assured as an insurer under any co-insurance clause, under such specific insurance), which said excess only is declared to be under the protection of this policy and subject to average aforesaid.

Other insurance permitted.

It is understood and agreed that this company shall not be liable for an amount exceeding 10 per cent of the amount of this policy for loss by any one fire.

OCCUPANCY CLAUSE.

Adopted January 11, 1906.

See also page 40.

Permission granted for the use of the premises as at present and for other purposes not any more hazardous, and to keep and use all articles and materials usual to the business conducted therein; but the use, handling or storing of benzine, benzole, gasoline, naphtha, calcium carbide or fireworks is prohibited unless a special permit is attached thereto.

FORM NO. 1.—PERMIT FOR OPENING IN PARTY WALLS WITH STANDARD IRON DOORS.

Adopted January 11, 1906.

See also page 34.

For and in consideration of $....... additional premium and of an agreement filed with The Chicago Board of Underwriters, "That before any openings shall be made in a wall all material necessary to protect such opening according to the specifications shall be in the building; that no openings shall be without the protection specified more than 24 hours; and that not more than two openings shall be unprotected at any one time."

Permission is hereby given to............to cut opening ....in..............wall between building No......... and .... as follows..................the same to be protected by double standard iron doors, constructed as per specifications on the back of this permit, and subject to inspection and approval when completed.

N. B.—All policies must have the above permit endorsed thereon.

SPECIFICATIONS FOR STANDARD IRON DOORS.

Doors to be equipped with approved automatic device for closing them in case of fire, and opening in wall to be protected within 24 hours after breaking wall.

Doors to be placed on either side of openings in fire walls, in Chicago, outside the district specified in the district for vault doors.

Doors to be made of No. 12 plate iron, with a continuous 2x2x¼ inch angle iron frame, firmly riveted. Two panel doors must have proper cross bars, must be fastened together with hooks, bolts or spring catches at top and bottom, and must have not less than two lever bars.

All doors must be hung on iron frames of ⅜x4 inch iron with 1½x1½x¼ inch angle iron riveted on the back, to be securely bolted together through the wall, and swing on three hinges. Doors must fit close to frame all around. Sill between doors must be iron, brick or stone, and not less than two (2) inches above the floor on each side of the opening. Lintel over door must be brick, iron or stone.

Floors of the basement where doors are to swing must be stone or concrete, in no case must it be wood.

If doors are sliding, they should be of same thickness of iron as above, constructed so as to run in iron channel bar top and bottom, bolted to bar frame; sheaves to be anti-friction and catch pin and drop catches front and rear bolted to frame so as to bind door to wall.

NOTE.—For working specifications see rules and requirements of the National Board of Fire Underwriters for the construction and installation of fire doors.

FORM NO. 2.—PERMIT FOR OPENINGS IN PARTY WALLS WITH VAULT IRON DOORS.

Adopted January 11, 1906.

See also page 34.

For and in consideration of $........additional premium and of an agreement filed with The Chicago Board of Underwriters, "That before any openings shall be made in a wall all materials necessary to protect such opening according to the specifications shall be in the building; that no openings shall be without the protection specified more than 24 hours; and that not more than two openings shall be unprotected at any one time."

Permission is hereby given to........to cut opening........ in...........wall between building No. .... and .... as follows.................... the same to be protected by double vault iron doors, constructed as per specifications on the back of this permit, and subject to inspection and approval when completed.

N. B.—All policies must have the above permit endorsed thereon.

SPECIFICATIONS FOR VAULT IRON DOORS.

Doors to be equipped with approved automatic device for closing them in case of fire, and opening in wall to be protected within 24 hours after breaking wall; also assured shall enter into contract with firm installing device that said firm will inspect it once a month and report condition of device to this association.

Doors to be placed on each side of openings in fire walls, in the district bounded by Harrison street on south, Chicago River on north and west, and Lake Michigan on east.

Doors to be made of 3-16 inch plate iron, with continuous 2x2x⅜ inch angle iron bolt frame, firmly riveted around inner edge. Doors must have proper cross bars, must be fastened together with hooks, bolts or spring catches at top and bottom, and must have not less than two lever bars.

Frames to be made of 4x⅜ inch iron, with 1½x1½ inch angle iron on back, each door to swing on three hinges and tongue into groove in frame on hinge side, right-hand door to fold over left-hand door, bottom piece of frame to be of 2x⅜ inch iron projecting above floor. Sill between doors must be iron, brick or stone, and rise not less than two (2) inches above the floor on each side of the opening. Lintel over door must be brick, iron or stone.

Each set of frames to be connected by proper bars of 1⅛x⅜ inch iron. Floor of the basement where doors are to swing must be stone or concrete; in no case must it be wood.

If doors are sliding, they should be of same thickness of iron as above, constructed so as to run in iron channel bar top and bottom, bolted to wall frame; sheaves to be anti-friction and catch pin and drop catches front and rear bolted to frame so as to bind door to wall.

NOTE.—For working specifications see rules and requirements of the National Board of Fire Underwriters for the construction and installation of fire doors.

PAPER HANGERS, PAINTERS AND DECORATORS' TOOLS AND IMPLEMENTS—FLOATER.

Adopted January 11, 1906.

Rate under this form, 2½ per cent. Advance applies.

$........On all tools, implements, appliances and apparatus used in business as................while located anywhere in Cook County, Illinois, except in the place of business of the assured.

It is hereby declared and agreed that in case the property aforesaid in all the places or limits included in this insurance shall, at the breaking out of any fire or fires, be collectively of greater value than the sum insured, then this company shall pay and make good such a portion only of the loss or damage as the

sum hereby insured shall bear to the whole value of the property aforesaid at the time when such fire or fires shall first happen.

It is understood and agreed that this company shall not be liable for an amount exceeding its proportion of $2,500 for loss by any one fire.

GENERAL PATTERNS FLOATER.

Adopted January 11, 1906.

Rate, 2 per cent. Advance applies.

$........On their wood and metal patterns and appurtenances, all while contained in any foundry or machine shop, except the premises of the assured in Cook County, Illinois.

In consideration of the rate at which this policy is written it is expressly stipulated and made a condition of this contract that this company shall be liable for no greater proportion of any loss than the amount hereby insured bears to the actual cash value of the property described herein at the time when such loss shall happen, nor for more than the proportion which this policy bears to the total contributing insurance thereon.

But it is at the same time declared and agreed that if any specific property described above, included in the terms of this policy, shall at the time of any fire be insured in this or any other company, this policy shall not extend to cover the same, excepting only as far as relates to any excess of value beyond the amount of such specific insurance, and shall not be liable for any loss unless the amount of such loss shall exceed the amount of such specific insurance (disregarding the liability of the assured as an insurer under any co-insurance clause, under such specific insurance), which said excess only is declared to be under the protection of this policy and subject to average aforesaid.

Other insurance permitted.

It is understood and agreed that this company shall not be liable for an amount exceeding 30 per cent of the amount of this policy for loss by any one fire.

PIANO AND ORGAN FLOATER.

Adopted January 11, 1906.

Rate under this form, 3 per cent. Advance applies.

$........On Pianos and Organs and stools, their own or in which they may have an interest, or for which they may be liable while contained in any building in Cook County, Illinois, except general storage warehouses, and the premises of the assured.

In consideration of the rate at which this policy is written it is expressly stipulated and made a condition of this contract that this company shall be liable for no greater proportion of any loss than the amount hereby insured bears to the actual cash value of the property described herein at the time when such loss shall happen, nor for more than the proportion which this policy bears to the total contributing insurance thereon.

But it is at the same time declared and agreed that if any specific property described above, included in the terms of this policy, shall at the time of any fire be insured in this or any other company, this policy shall not extend to cover the same, excepting only as far as relates to any excess of value beyond the amount of such specific insurance, and shall not be liable for any loss unless the amount of such loss shall exceed the amount of such specific insurance (disregarding the liability of the assured as an insurer under any co-insurance clause, under such specific insurance), which said excess only is declared to be under the protection of this policy and subject to average aforesaid.

Other insurance permitted.

It is understood and agreed that this company shall not be liable for an amount exceeding twenty per cent of the amount of this policy for loss by any one fire.

PIANO AND ORGAN FLOATER.—(Preferred Risks.)

Adopted January 11, 1906.

Rate under this form, 1 per cent. Advance applies.

$........On Pianos and Organs and stools, their own or in which they may have an interest, or for which they may be liable while contained in any building in Cook County, Illinois, while the same is occupied exclusively for either or all of the following named purposes: Apartment House, Charitable Institution, Church, Club House, Dwelling, Flats, Hall without scenery, Offices, Private Boarding House, Public Institution, School House, Stores, grade floor or below and dwelling, flats or apartment house above.

In consideration of the rate at which this policy is written it is expressly stipulated and made a condition of this contract that this company shall be liable for no greater proportion of any loss than the amount hereby insured bears to the actual cash value of the property described herein at the time when such loss shall happen, nor for more than the proportion which this policy bears to the total contributing insurance thereon.

But it is at the same time declared and agreed, that if any specific property described above included in the terms of this policy shall, at the time of any fire, be insured in this or any other company, this policy shall not extend to cover the same, excepting only as far as relates to any excess of value beyond the amount of such specific insurance, and shall not be liable for any loss unless the amount of such loss shall exceed the amount of such specific insurance (disregarding the liability of the assured as an insurer under any co-insurance clause, under such specific insurance), which said excess only is declared to be under the protection of this policy and subject to average aforesaid.

Other insurance permitted.

It is understood and agreed that this company shall not be liable for an amount exceeding twenty per cent of the amount of this policy for loss by any one fire.

PRINTERS' BENZINE WARRANTY.

Adopted January 11, 1906

See also page 31.

Warranted by the assured that no benzine, gasoline, mineral turpentine, naphtha or other product of petroleum, except refined coal oil of lawful test, shall be used or kept on the premises during the life of this policy.

PROPERTY UPON WHICH THE ASSURED MAY LOAN MONEY—FLOATER.

Adopted January 11, 1906.

Rate under this form, 4 per cent. Advance applies.

$........On household furniture, useful and ornamental, silver and plated ware, printed books, musical instruments and general merchandise upon which the assured may have loaned money, either for himself or parties whom he represents, in sums not exceeding $150, all while contained in different buildings in Cook County, Illinois.

It is understood and agreed that in case of loss on property described, contained in any one of the places above referred to, that no loss in any one of the said places shall exceed the sum of $150 under this policy, or the actual amount due the assured, where payments have been made as evidenced by his notes and mortgages.

It is provided further, in event of loss, that this company, upon payment to the mortgagees of the sum due under this mortgage, shall fully be subrogated to the mortgagee's rights and interests.

Other concurrent insurance permitted.

In consideration of the rate at which this policy is written it is expressly stipulated and made a condition of this contract that this company shall be liable for no greater proportion of any loss than the amount hereby insured bears to eighty per cent of the actual cash value of the property described herein at the time when such loss shall happen, nor for more than the proportion which this policy bears to the total contributing insurance thereon.

REGALIA AND PARAPHERNALIA FLOATER.

Adopted October 19, 1906.

Rate, 2 per cent. Advance applies.

$........On regalia and paraphernalia, equipment of all kinds, including trunks, valises and suit cases, jewels, banners and emblems, useful and ornamental, initiating apparatus and appurtenances in any building in the County of Cook, State of Illinois.

But it is at the same time declared and agreed, that if any specific property described above included in the terms of this

PRIVATE CONVEYANCE FLOATER (OTHER THAN AUTOMOBILES).

For use in insuring horses and/or vehicles (other than automobiles) used for pleasure driving or riding only.

Rate on this form not to be less than that of the place where the property is usually housed. *which must always be stated in the form*, nor less than one and one-half per cent. (1½%) per annum, long term rate pro rata of the annual rate.

$......On driving and/or riding outfit, consisting of horses, vehicles (other than automobiles), harness, saddles, trappings, robes, covers, feed and stable utensils, while contained in........
...................................or elsewhere in the State of Illinois, either in or out of building.

In case of loss no one animal to be valued at more than...... dollars.

In consideration of the rate at which this policy is written it is expressly stipulated and made a condition of this contract that this company shall be liable for no greater proportion of any loss than the amount hereby insured bears to the actual cash value of the property described herein at the time when such loss shall happen, nor for more than the proportion which this policy bears to the total contributing insurance thereon.

But it is at the same time declared and agreed, that if any specific property described above included in the terms of this policy, shall, at the time of any fire, be insured in this or any other company, this policy shall not extend to cover the same, excepting only as far as relates to any excess of value beyond the amount of such specific insurance, and shall not be liable for any loss unless the amount of such loss shall exceed the amount of such specific insurance (disregarding the liability of the assured as an insurer under any co-insurance clause, under such specific insurance) which said excess only is declared to be under the protection of this policy and subject to average aforesaid.

Other insurance permitted.

This policy shall cover any direct loss or damage caused by Lightning, except loss or damage to electrical apparatus and machinery and connections in use (meaning thereby the commonly accepted use of the term lightning, and in no case to include loss or damage by cyclone, tornado or windstorm), not exceeding the sum insured, nor the interest of the insured in the property, and subject in all other respects to the terms and conditions of this policy. Provided, however, if there shall be any other fire insurance on said property, this company shall be liable only pro rata with such other insurance for any direct loss by lightning, whether such other insurance be against direct loss by lightning or not.

policy shall, at the time of any fire, be insured in this or any other company, this policy shall not extend to cover the same, excepting only as far as relates to any excess of value beyond the amount of such specific insurance, and shall not be liable for any loss unless the amount of such loss shall exceed the amount of such specific insurance (disregarding the liability of the assured as an insurer under any co-insurance clause, under such specific insurance), which said excess only is declared to be under the protection of this policy and subject to average aforesaid.

In consideration of the rate at which this policy is written it is expressly stipulated and made a condition of this contract that this company shall be liable for no greater proportion of any loss than the amount hereby insured bears to one hundred per cent of the actual cash value of the property described herein at the time when such loss shall happen, nor for more than the proportion which this policy bears to the total contributing insurance thereon.

Other insurance permitted.

REMOVAL PERMIT.

Adopted January 11, 1906.

See also page 43.

Permission is hereby given during the period of thirty days from date hereof to remove the property insured under this policy from .... to .... Illinois.

It is understood and agreed that during such removal this policy shall attach in both locations in proportion as the value of the property insured in each bears to such value in both localities, that from and after the expiration of said thirty days and prior thereto, if the removal shall have been completed, this policy shall attach in the new location only, and the effect of the average clause be discontinued, and that additional premium pro rata of increase in rate, if any, in the new location shall be paid within thirty days from this date.

FORM NO. 1 FOR INSURANCE OF RENTAL VALUES.

Adopted April 12, 1906.

When this form is used the rate may be 25 per cent off the Building Rate.

$...... ..On rental value of the .... story .... building, with .... roof, while occupied by the assured, situate...................
....
....

It is understood and agreed that in case the above named building, or any occupied part thereof, shall be rendered untenantable by fire, this company shall be liable to the assured for the actual loss of rental value ensuing therefrom, not exceeding the sum

insured, based upon the actual rental value of that part of the building actually occupied by assured at the time of the fire. Loss to be computed from the date of the occurrence of said fire, and to be determined by the time it would require to put the premises in tenantable condition.

Other concurrent insurance permitted.

The assured stipulates and agrees to carry insurance on said rental value in an amount equal to not less than *Seventy-five per cent* of the actual annual rental value of said premises, and it is understood and agreed that if at the time of fire, the aggregate amount of insurance upon said rental value shall be less than *Seventy-five per cent* of said total rental value, the insured shall be held to be an insurer in the amount of such deficiency, and in that capacity shall bear a proportionate share of the loss.

FORM NO. 2 FOR INSURANCE OF RENTAL VALUES.

Adopted April 12, 1906.

When this form is used the rate may be 33 1-3 per cent off the Building Rate.

$........On rental value of the .... story .... building, with ....
roof, while occupied by the assured, situate....................
....
....

It is understood and agreed that in case the above named building, or any occupied part thereof, shall be rendered untenantable by fire, this company shall be liable to the assured for the actual loss of rental value ensuing therefrom, not exceeding the sum insured, based upon the actual rental value of that part of the building actually occupied by assured at the time of the fire. Loss to be computed from the date of the occurrence of said fire, and to be determined by the time it would require to put the premises in tenantable condition.

Other concurrent insurance permitted.

It is understood and agreed that in case of loss, this company shall not be liable in excess of the proportion that the sum insured under this policy bears to the actual annual rental value of the premises at the time of the fire.

FORM NO. 1 FOR INSURANCE ON RENTS.

Adopted January 11, 1906.

See also page 41.

Form No. 1. For Insurance on Rents. When this form is used the rate may be 25 per cent less than the building rate.
$........On rents of the .... story ....building, with ....roof, situate........................

It is understood and agreed that in case the above named building, or any part thereof, shall be rendered untenantable by fire, this company shall be liable to the assured for the actual loss of rent ensuing therefrom, not exceeding the sum insured, based upon bona fide leases in force at the time of the fire. Loss to be computed from the date of the occurrence of said fire, and to be determined by the time it would require to put the premises in tenantable condition.

Other concurrent insurance permitted.

The assured stipulates and agrees to carry insurance on said rents in an amount equal to not less than seventy-five per cent of the actual annual rents of said premises, and it is understood and agreed that if at the time of fire the aggregate amount of insurance upon said rents shall be less than 75 per cent of said total rents, the insured shall be held to be an insurer in the amount of such deficiency, and in that capacity shall bear a proportionate share of the loss.

FORM NO. 2 FOR INSURANCE ON RENTS.

Adopted January 11, 1906.

See also page 41

When this form is used the rate may be 33 1-3 per cent less than the building rate.

$........On rents, of the ....story .... building, with .... roof, situate ....

It is understood and agreed that in case the above named building, or any part thereof, shall be rendered untenantable by fire, this company shall be liable to the assured for the actual loss of rent ensuing therefrom, not exceeding the sum insured, based upon bona fide leases in force at the time of the fire. Loss to be computed from the date of the occurrence of said fire, and to be determined by the time it would require to put the premises in tenantable condition.

Other concurrent insurance permitted.

It is understood and agreed that in case of loss this company shall only be liable in the proportion that the sum insured under this policy bears to the actual annual rental of the premises at the time of the fire.

SAFES AND VAULTS.—Property in.

WARRANTY. Adopted January 11, 1906 Amended October 11, 1906.

Form of warranty to be used on policies covering property in and out of safes and vaults when a reduction from the published contents rate is made on property so insured:

In consideration of a reduction in the premium charged for this policy, it is hereby stipulated and the assured warrants that

not less than .... per cent of the entire value of the property covered by this policy shall be at all times contained in safes or vaults, and in event of loss or damage adjustment shall be made on that basis:

SCALE OF DEDUCTIONS.
(To be detached.)

10 per cent warranted deduct			5 per cent from rate.			
20	"	"	"	10	"	"	"
30	"	"	"	15	"	"	"
40	"	"	"	20	"	"	"
50	"	"	"	25	"	"	"
60	"	"	"	30	"	"	"
70	"	"	"	35	"	"	"
80	"	"	"	40	"	"	"
90	"	"	"	45	"	"	"
100	"	"	"	50	"	"	"

SALOON FURNITURE AND FIXTURE FLOATER.

Adopted January 11, 1906.

Rate 2½ per cent   Advance applies.

$........On saloon and bar room furniture and fixtures, including cash registers, ice boxes, pumps, glassware, mirrors, pictures, engravings, and their frames (at not exceeding cost price), show cases, back cases, counters, tables, chairs, stoves and pipes, implements and all tools usually kept in saloons, including awnings and signs, pool and billiard tables, balls, cues, racks and covers, all while contained in or on any building in Cook County, Ill., excluding their Brewery premises, and all warehouses occupied for storage of furniture and fixtures and all manufacturing plants of any kind or nature.

In consideration of the rate at which this policy is written it is expressly stipulated and made a condition of this contract that this company shall be liable for no greater proportion of any loss than the amount hereby insured bears to the actual cash value of the property described herein at the time when such loss shall happen, nor for more than the proportion which this policy bears to the total contributing insurance thereon.

But it is at the same time declared and agreed, that if any specific parcel of goods included in the terms of this policy, or such goods in any specified building or buildings, place or places, within the limits of this insurance shall, at the time of any fire, be insured in this or any other company, this policy shall not extend to cover the same, excepting only as far as relates to any excess of value beyond the amount of such specific insurance, and shall not be liable for any loss unless the amount of such loss shall exceed the amount of such specific insurance (disregarding the liability of the assured as an insurer under any

co-insurance clause, under such specific insurance), which said excess only is declared to be under the protection of this policy and subject to average aforesaid.

It being the true intent and meaning of this agreement that this company shall not be liable for any loss unless the amount of such loss shall exceed the amount of such specific insurance, and then only for such excess, which said excess shall be subject to average as above.

Other insurance permitted.

It is understood and agreed that this company shall not be liable for an amount exceeding ten per cent of the amount of this policy for loss by any one fire.

STORAGE CHARGES IN GRAIN ELEVATORS AND STORAGE WAREHOUSES.

Adopted January 11, 1906.

See also pages 41 and 44.

Rate under this form 90 per cent of the contents rate.

$........ on storage charges on property of others while stored in .... situate ....

The liability of this company under this policy shall not exceed its proportionate part of the storage charges, not otherwise insured, accrued and unpaid on property stored in the building described, at the time of the occurrence of fire therein that cannot be collected from the owners thereof without legal process made good from value of property saved, or from insurance covering property destroyed, issued to or payable to this assured, nor exceeding the value of or damage to any lot of property damaged or destroyed and not in any event exceeding the sum insured.

It is understood and agreed that this company shall on the payment of the loss be subrogated to the extent of such payment to all right of recovery by the assured against the owners of the property stored for unpaid storage charges, that assured shall disclose the owners thereof if within his knowledge or power, and shall assign such claim and transfer all securities held by him to secure the payment thereof, but the collection of such claim shall be at the proper costs and charges of this company.

Other insurance permitted.

In consideration of the rate at which this policy is written it is expressly stipulated and made a condition of this contract that this company shall be liable for no greater proportion of any loss than the amount hereby insured bears to eighty per cent of the actual cash value of the property described herein at the time when such loss shall happen, nor for more than the proportion which this policy bears to the total contributing insurance thereon. If this policy be divided into two or more items, the foregoing conditions shall apply to each item separately.

TAILOR'S FLOATING POLICY.

Adopted January 11, 1906.

Rate under this form, 2½ per cent Advance applies.

$........On clothing manufactured and in process of manufacture, and materials for same, while in the hands of tailors making it, in any building in the County of Cook, State of Illinois, excepting the building occupied by the assured as a place of business.

It is understood and agreed that the Tailor's work or wages for same are not insured under this policy.

It is further understood and agreed that if, at the time of any fire, the value of the entire property herein described exceeds the sum insured under this policy, then and in that case this company shall be liable only for such proportion of loss as the sum insured hereunder bears to the total value of the said property, less the amount of all specific insurance resting thereon (disregarding the liability of the assured as an insurer under any co-insurance clause under such specific insurance); provided, however, that if there be any specific insurance upon the property destroyed or damaged, made by the assured, or by the Tailor for his benefit, this company shall not contribute with such specific insurance, but such specific insurance shall be first exhausted; and provided, further, that in no event shall this company be liable for more than 10 per cent of the sum insured hereunder for loss in any one building.

Other insurance permitted.

TAILOR'S MERCHANDISE POLICY.—Specific Form.

Adopted January 11, 1906.

$........On clothing manufactured or in process of manufacture, and materials for same, while in the hands of........
................Tailor, and contained in the ....
situate..........................

It is understood and agreed that the Tailor's work or wages for same is not insured under this policy; and it is further understood and agreed that if the assured shall have any insurance on the property herein described, effected under Floating Policies, providing for non-contribution with specific insurance, the same shall not be held to contribute, in case of loss, with this policy.

In consideration of the rate at which this policy is written it is expressly stipulated and made a condition of this contract that this company shall be liable for no greater proportion of any loss than the amount hereby insured bears to eighty per cent of the actual cash value of the property described herein at the time when such loss shall happen, nor for more than the proportion which this policy bears to the total contributing insurance thereon. If this policy be divided into two or more items, the foregoing conditions shall apply to each item separately.

Other insurance permitted.

FORM FOR TEAMING OUTFIT FLOATER.

Adopted January 11, 1906.

Rate under this form, 2½ per cent   Advance applies.

$...... On teaming outfit, including horses, vehicles, harness, trappings, robes, covers, feed and stable utensils, and on merchandise contained in vehicles, while contained in any private barn, livery or boarding stable, or wagon repair shop, or in transit in Cook County, Illinois, except the stables of the assured.

In case of loss no one animal to be valued at more than .... dollars.

In consideration of the rate at which this policy is written it is expressly stipulated and made a condition of this contract that this company shall be liable for no greater proportion of any loss than the amount hereby insured bears to the actual cash value of the property described herein at the time when such loss shall happen, nor for more than the proportion which this policy bears to the total contributing insurance thereon.

But it is at the same time declared and agreed, that if any specific property described above included in the terms of this policy shall, at the time of any fire, be insured in this or any other company, this policy shall not extend to cover the same, excepting only as far as relates to any excess of value beyond the amount of such specific insurance, and shall not be liable for any loss unless the amount of such loss shall exceed the amount of such specific insurance (disregarding the liability of the assured as an insurer under any co-insurance clause, under such specific insurance), which said excess only is declared to be under the protection of this policy and subject to average aforesaid.

Other insurance permitted.

FORM FOR FLOATER ON MERCHANDISE IN HANDS OF TEAMSTERS, Including Stables of the Assured.

Adopted January 11, 1906.

Rate under this form 2½ per cent.   **Advance applies.**

$........ On merchandise and other property of others for which he may be legally liable contained in vehicles, while in any private barn, livery or boarding stable, or wagon repair shop, or in transit in Cook County, Illinois, including the stables of the assured.

In consideration of the rate at which this policy is written it is expressly stipulated and made a condition of this contract that this company shall be liable for no greater proportion of any loss than the amount hereby insured bears to the actual cash value of the property described herein at the time when such loss shall happen, nor for more than the proportion which this policy bears to the total contributing insurance thereon.

But it is at the same time declared and agreed, that if any specific property described above included in the terms of this policy shall, at the time of any fire, be insured in this or any other company, this policy shall not extend to cover the same, excepting only as far as relates to any excess of value beyond the amount of such specific insurance, and shall not be liable for any loss unless the amount of such loss shall exceed the amount of such specific insurance (disregarding the liability of the assured as an insurer under any co-insurance clause, under such specific insurance), which said excess only is declared to be under the protection of this policy and subject to average aforesaid.

Other insurance permitted.

FORM NO. 1.—RAILROAD AND STEAMBOAT WAREHOUSE FLOATER.—Limited.

Adopted January 11, 1906.

Rate, 1¼ per cent. Advance applies.

$........On merchandise (including packages) consisting principally of ....
....
excluding petroleum and its liquid products, the property of the assured, or held by the assured in trust or on commission or on joint account with others, or sold but not delivered, while in the possession of any common carrier, either while in any building or while in transit in or on any of the streets, yards, wharves, piers and bulkheads, and while in cars on tracks, when at assured's risk, in Cook County, Illinois, except in the district known as the Union Stock Yards, Chicago, bounded on the east by Halsted Street, north by 39th Street, west by Ashland Avenue to 45th Street, south by 45th Street to Loomis Street, west by Loomis Street to 47th Street and south by 47th Street to Halsted Street.

In consideration of the rate at which this policy is written it is expressly stipulated and made a condition of this contract that this company shall be liable for no greater proportion of any loss than the amount hereby insured bears to the actual cash value of the property described herein at the time when such loss shall happen, nor for more than the proportion which this policy bears to the total contributing insurance thereon.

But it is at the same time declared and agreed, that if any specific parcel of goods included in the terms of this policy, or such goods in any specified building or buildings, place or places, within the limits of this insurance, shall, at the time of any fire, be insured in this or any other company, this policy shall not extend to cover the same, excepting only as far as relates to any excess of value beyond the amount of such specific insurance, and shall not be liable for any loss unless the amount of such loss shall exceed the amount

of such specific insurance (disregarding the liability of the assured as an insurer under any co-insurance clause, under such specific insurance), which said **excess** only is declared to be under the protection of this policy and subject to average aforesaid. It being the true intent and meaning of this agreement that this Company shall not be liable for any loss unless the amount of such loss shall exceed the amount of such specific insurance, and then only for such excess, which said excess shall be subject to average as above.

If this Company shall claim that any person or corporation, private or municipal, is responsible for the loss, whether caused by the act or neglect of such person or corporation, or otherwise, this Company shall, on the payment of the loss, be subrogated to the extent of such payment to all right of recovery by the insured for the loss, and such right shall be assigned to this Company by the insured on receiving such payment.

This policy does not cover in whole or in part, goods on which at the time of any fire there may be any marine, inland or transportation insurance.

Other insurance permitted.

It is understood and agreed that this Company shall not be liable for an amount exceeding 25 per cent of the amount of this policy for loss by any one fire, in any one building or place.

FORM NO. 2, RAILROAD AND STEAMBOAT WAREHOUSE FLOATER.—Unlimited.

Adopted January 11, 1906.

Rate 2 per cent **Advance applies.**

$........On merchandise (including packages) consisting principally of ....
..,...
excluding petroleum and its liquid products, the property of the assured, or held by the assured in trust or on commission or on joint account with others, or sold but not delivered, while in the possession of any common carrier, either while in any building or while in transit in or on any of the streets, yards, wharves, piers and bulk-heads, and while in cars on tracks, when at assured's risk, in Cook County, Illinois, except in the district known as the Union Stock Yards, Chicago, bounded on the east by Halsted Street, north by 39th Street, west by Ashland Avenue to 45th Street, south by 45th Street to Loomis Street, west by Loomis Street to 47th Street, and south by 47th Street to Halsted Street.

In consideration of the rate at which this policy is written it is expressly stipulated and made a condition of this contract that this company shall be liable for no greater proportion of any loss than the amount hereby insured bears to the actual cash value of the property described herein at the time when such loss shall happen, nor for more than the proportion which this policy bears to the total contributing insurance thereon.

But it is at the same time declared and agreed, that if any specific parcel of goods included in the terms of this policy, or such goods in any specified building or buildings, place or places. within the limits of this insurance, shall at the time of any fire be insured in this or any other company, this policy shall not extend to cover the same, excepting only as far as relates to any excess of value beyond the amount of such specific insurance, and shall not be liable for any loss unless the amount of such loss shall exceed the amount of such specific insurance (disregarding the liability of the assured as an insurer under any co-insurance clause under such specific insurance), which said excess only is declared to be under the protection of this policy and subject to average aforesaid. It being the true intent and meaning of this agreement that this company shall not be liable for any loss unless the amount of such loss shall exceed the amount of such specific insurance, and then only for such excess, which said excess shall be subject to average as above.

If this company shall claim that any person or corporation, private or municipal, is responsible for the loss, whether caused by the act or neglect of such person or corporation, or otherwise this company shall, on the payment of the loss, be subrogated to the extent of such payment to all right of recovery by the insured for the loss, and such right shall be assigned to this company by the insured on receiving such payment.

This policy does not cover in whole or in part, goods on which at the time of any fire there may be any marine, inland or transportation insurance.

Other insurance permitted

FORM NO. 1, RAILROAD AND STEAMBOAT WAREHOUSE METAL FLOATER.— Limited.

Adopted January 11, 1906.

Rate 1 per cent without advance.

$........On merchandise (including packages) consisting exclusively of copper, lead, tin, spelter, brass and other base metals, the property of the assured or held by the assured in trust or on commission or on joint account with others or sold but not delivered, while in the possession of any common carrier, either while in any building or while in transit in or on any of the streets, yards, wharves, piers and bulkheads, and while in cars on tracks, when at assured's risk, in Cook County, Illinois, except in the district known as the Union Stock Yards, Chicago, bounded on the east by Halsted Street, north by 39th Street, west by Ashland Avenue to 45th Street, south by 45th Street to Loomis Street, west by Loomis Street to 47th Street and south by 47th Street to Halsted Street.

In consideration of the rate at which this policy is written it is expressly stipulated and made a condition of this contract that this Company shall be liable for no greater proportion of

any loss than the amount hereby insured bears to the....per cent of the actual cash value of the property described herein at the time when such loss shall happen, nor for more than the proportion which this policy bears to the total contributing insurance thereon.

If this policy be divided into two or more items the foregoing conditions shall apply to each item separately.

But it is at the same time declared and agreed, that if any specific parcel of goods included in the terms of this policy or such goods in any specified building or buildings, place or places, within the limits of this insurance, shall at the time of any fire, be insured in this or any other Company, this policy shall not extend to cover the same excepting only as far as relates to any excess of value beyond the amount of such specific insurance, and shall not be liable for any loss, unless the amount of such loss shall exceed the amount of such specific insurance (disregarding the liability of the assured as an insurer under any coinsurance clause under such specific insurance), which said excess only is declared to be under the protection of this policy and subject to average aforesaid. It being the true intent and meaning of this agreement that this Company shall not be liable for any loss, unless the amount of such loss shall exceed the amount of specific insurance and then only for such excess, which said excess shall be subject to average as above.

If this Company shall claim that any person or corporation, private or municipal, is responsible for the loss, whether caused by the act or neglect of such person or corporation, or otherwise, this Company shall on the payment of the loss, be subrogated to the extent of such payment to all right of recovery by the insured for the loss, and such right shall be assigned to this Company by the insured on receiving such payment.

This policy does not cover in whole or in part, goods on which at the time of any fire there may be any marine, inland or transportation insurance.

Other insurance permitted.

It is understood and agreed that this Company shall not be liable for an amount exceeding 25 per cent of the amount of this policy for loss by any one fire, in any one building or place.

FORM NO. 2, RAILROAD AND STEAMBOAT WAREHOUSE METAL FLOATER.—Unlimited.

Adopted January 11, 1906.

Rate 1½ per cent without advance.

$........On merchandise (including packages) consisting exclusively of copper, lead, tin, spelter, brass and other base metals, the property of the assured or held by the assured in trust or on commission or on joint account with others or sold but not delivered, while in the possession of any common carrier, either while in any building or while in transit in or on any of the

streets, yards, wharves, piers and bulkheads, and while in cars on tracks, when at assured's risk, in Cook County, Illinois, except in the district known as the Union Stock Yards, Chicago, bounded on the east by Halsted Street, north by 39th Street, west by Ashland Avenue to 45th Street, south by 45th Street to Loomis Street, west by Loomis Street to 47th Street and south by 47th Street to Halsted Street.

In consideration of the rate at which this policy is written it is expressly stipulated and made a condition of this contract that this Company shall be liable for no greater proportion of any loss than the amount hereby insured bears to the....per cent of the actual cash value of the property described herein at the time when such loss shall happen, nor for more than the proportion which this policy bears to the total contributing insurance thereon.

But it is at the same time declared and agreed, that if any specific parcel of goods included in the terms of this policy or such goods in any specified building or buildings, place or places, within the limits of this insurance, shall at the time of any fire be insured in this or any other Company, this policy shall not extend to cover the same excepting only as far as relates to any excess of value beyond the amount of such specific insurance, and shall not be liable for any loss, unless the amount of such loss shall exceed the amount of such specific insurance (disregarding the liability of the assured as an insurer under any co-insurance clause under such specific insurance), which said excess only is declared to be under the protection of this policy and subject to average aforesaid. It being the true intent and meaning of this agreement that this Company shall not be liable for any loss, unless the amount of such loss shall exceed the amount of specific insurance, and then only for such excess, which said excess shall be subject to average as above.

If this Company shall claim that any person or corporation, private or municipal, is responsible for the loss, whether caused by the act or neglect of such person or corporation, or otherwise, this Company shall on the payment of the loss, be subrogated to the extent of such payment to all right of recovery by the insured for the loss, and such right shall be assigned to this Company by the insured on receiving such payment.

This policy does not cover in whole or in part, goods on which at the time of any fire there may be any marine, inland or transportation insurance.

Other insurance permitted.

RAILROAD TIES AND TELEGRAPH POLES.—Floater.

Adopted January 11, 1906.

Rate 2½ per cent   Advance applies.

$........On Railroad Ties and Telegraph Poles, their own or held by them in trust, or on commission, or sold but not

delivered, all while contained in yards anywhere in Cook County, State of Illinois, excluding the premises of the assured.

It is hereby declared and agreed that in case the property aforesaid in all the buildings, places or limits included in this insurance, shall, at the breaking out of any fire or fires, be collectively of greater value than the sum insured, then this Company shall pay and make good such a portion only of the loss or damage as the sum hereby insured shall bear to the whole value of the property aforesaid at the time when such fire or fires shall first happen.

But, it is at the same time declared and agreed, that if any specific, parcel of goods included in the terms of this policy, or such goods in any specified building or buildings, lace or places, within the limits of this insurance, shall at the time of any fire be insured in this or any other Company, this policy shall not extend to cover the same, excepting only as far as relates to any excess of value beyond the amount of such specific insurance and shall not be liable for any loss unless the amount of such loss shall exceed the amount of such specific insurance which said excess only is declared to be under the protection of this policy and subject to average aforesaid.

It being the true intent and meaning of this agreement that this Company shall not be liable for any loss, unless the amount of such loss shall exceed the amount of such specific insurance and then only for such excess, which said excess shall be subject to average as above.

Other insurance permitted without notice until required.

SODA FOUNTAINS.—Floater.

Adopted January 11, 1906.

Rate 2½ per cent **Advance applies.**

$........On Soda Fountains, apparatus and accessories, their own or in which they may have an interest as part owners, mortgagees or otherwise, while contained in any building—except their own premises, all general storage warehouses and all manufacturing plants of any kind or nature—in Cook County, Illinois.

In consideration of the rate at which this policy is written it is expressly stipulated and made a condition of this contract that this Company shall be liable for no greater proportion of any loss than the amount hereby insured bears to the actual cash value of the property described herein at the time when such loss shall happen, nor for more than the proportion which this policy bears to the total contributing insurance thereon.

But it is at the same time declared and agreed, that if any specific property described above, included in the terms of this policy, shall, at the time of any fire, be insured in this or any other Company, this policy shall not extend to cover the same, excepting only as far as relates to any excess of value beyond the

amount of such specific insurance, and shall not be liable for any loss unless the amount of such loss shall exceed the amount of such specific insurance (disregarding the liability of the assured as an insurer under any co-insurance clause, under such specific insurance), which said excess only is declared to be under the protection of this policy and subject to average aforesaid.

Other insurance permitted.

It is understood and agreed that this Company shall not be liable for an amount exceeding ten per cent of the amount of this policy for loss by any one fire.

SPRINKLER MAINTENANCE CLAUSE.

Adopted January 11, 1906.

See also page 43

In consideration of the reduction in premium paid for this policy for protection of the premises by automatic sprinklers, it is hereby made a condition of this policy that, in so far as the Sprinkler System and water supplies therefor are within the control of the assured, due diligence shall be used by the assured in maintaining the automatic sprinkler equipment in complete working order, during the full term of this insurance, provided, that for the purpose of making emergency repairs the water may be shut off for not exceeding twelve hours at any one time without notice. Conditioned, that if the water be shut off between the hours of 7 p. m. and 7 a. m., with the knowledge of the assured, a watchman shall be kept on each floor of the premises, controlled by the assured, during such time, and provided further, that the water shall not be shut off for more than twelve hours at any one time without notice to and the consent of this company in writing.

STREETS WESTERN STABLE CAR LINE.—Floater.

(Covering outside any building.)

Adopted January 11, 1906.

Rate 75c. Advance applies.

$........On Cars, their own or held by them in trust, or on commission, or for repairs, sold but not removed, when at the risk of the assured, while on tracks in the City of Chicago, Illinois, outside the territory mentioned in the "General Form" of policy covering property of assured and reading as follows: "Beginning at a point on the south line of 47th Street, about 208 feet west of the west line of the right of way of the Union Stock Yards and Transit Company's Railway (in Peoria Street), thence running south about 125 feet, thence west about 48 feet, thence south to the south line of 48th Street, thence west along said line of 48th Street about 180 feet, thence north to the south

line of 47th Street, thence east to the place of beginning." And it is expressly understood and agreed that in case of any loss this insurance shall not be held to contribute with the insurance written and covering under the "General Form" above referred to.

Claim for loss on any one car is limited to $400.

It is hereby declared and agreed that in case the property aforesaid in all the places or limits included in this insurance shall, at the breaking out of any fire or fires, be collectively of greater value than the sum insured, then this Company shall pay and make good such a portion only of the loss or damage as the sum hereby insured shall bear to the whole value of the property aforesaid at the time when such fire or fires shall first happen.

But it is at the same time declared and agreed, that if any specific parcel of goods included in the terms of this policy, in any place or places, within the limits of this insurance, shall, at the time of any fire, be insured in this or any other company, this policy shall not extend to cover the same, excepting only as far as relates to any excess of value beyond the amount of such specific insurance, and shall not be liable for any loss unless the amount of such loss shall exceed the amount of such specific insurance, which said excess only is declared to be under the protection of this policy and subject to average aforesaid. If this Company shall claim that any person or corporation, private or municipal, is responsible for the loss, whether caused by the act or neglect by such person or corporation, or otherwise, this Company shall, on the payment of the loss be subrogated to the extent of such payment to all right of recovery by the insured for the loss, and such right shall be assigned to this Company by the assured on receiving such payment.

Other insurance permitted without notice until required.

THOMSON & TAYLOR SPICE CO.—Floater.

Adopted January 11, 1906.

Rate 2½ per cent **Advance applies.**

$........On teaming outfit, including horses, vehicles, harness, trappings, robes, covers, feed and stable utensils, and on merchandise contained in vehicles while contained in any private barn, livery or boarding stable, or wagon repair shop or in transit in Cook County, Illinois, except the stables of the assured.

In case of loss no one animal to be valued at more than .... dollars.

It is hereby declared and agreed that in case the property aforesaid in all the buildings, places or limits included in this

insurance shall, at the breaking out of any fire or fires, be collectively of greater value than the sum insured, then this Company shall pay and make good such portion only of the loss or damage as the sum hereby insured shall bear to the whole value of the property aforesaid at the time when such fire or fires shall first happen.

But it is at the same time declared and agreed, that if any specific property described above included in the terms of this policy shall, at the time of any fire, be insured in this or any other company, this policy shall not extend to cover the same, excepting only as far as relates to any excess of value beyond the amount of such specific insurance, and shall not be liable for any loss unless the amount of such loss shall exceed the amount of such specific insurance, which said excess only is declared to be under the protection of this policy and subject to average aforesaid.

Other insurance permitted without notice until required.

TRANSMITTING TYPEWRITERS.—Floater.

Adopted January 11, 1906.

Rate 2½ per cent. Advance applies.

$........On transmitting typewriters, all while contained in any building in Cook County, except premises of assured and storage warehouses.

In consideration of the rate at which this policy is written it is expressly stipulated and made a condition of this contract that this company shall be liable for no greater proportion of any loss than the amount hereby insured bears to the actual cash value of the property described herein at the time when such loss shall happen, nor for more than the proportion which this policy bears to the total contributing insurance thereon.

But it is at the same time declared and agreed, that if any specific property described above included in the terms of this policy shall, at the time of any fire, be insured in this or any other company, this policy shall not extend to cover the same, excepting only as far as relates to any excess of value beyond the amount of such specific insurance, and shall not be liable for any loss unless the amount of such loss shall exceed the amount of such specific insurance (disregarding the liability of the assured as an insurer under any co-insurance clause, under such specific insurance), which said excess only is declared to be under the protection of this policy and subject to average aforesaid.

Other insurance permitted.

It is understood and agreed that this company shall not be liable for an amount exceeding 10 per cent of the amount of this policy for loss by any one fire.

USE AND OCCUPANCY, 150 DAYS.—Fixed Charges.

Adopted January 11, 1906.

See also page 2.
Rate, twice Building Rate.

$........On the use and occupancy of..................
....................situate................ Chicago, Illinois

The conditions of this contract of insurance are that if the buildings, or any part thereof, or the machinery contained therein, or any part thereof, shall be destroyed, or entirely disabled by fire occurring during the term, and under the conditions of this policy, so as to entirely prevent operating or carrying on the business, or if the buildings, or any part thereof, or the machinery contained therein, or any part thereof, shall be so damaged or disabled as to partially prevent operating or carrying on the business, then this Company shall be liable for its pro rata part of four-fifths of the loss sustained, ascertained and proven under the conditions of this policy on account of the following fixed charges, viz., salaries, wages, royalties, taxes, insurance and interest at the lawful rate on the cash value of the plant for such total or partial prevention not exceeding one-one hundred and fiftieth (1-150) part of the sum insured under this policy per day for total prevention, nor proportionately for partial prevention, for each working day (of 24 hours) of such total or partial prevention, and for not exceeding one hundred and fifty (150) of such working days, nor, in any event, exceeding the sum insured.

Loss, if any, to be computed from the day of the occurrence of any fire to the time when the said buildings and machinery therein could, with ordinary diligence and dispatch, be rebuilt, repaired or replaced, and not limited to the day of expiration named in this policy. For the purposes of this insurance it is agreed that the basis of claim hereunder shall not exceed the legal liability of the assured for salaries and wages of persons employed in connection with the business at the time of the fire, and for royalties not suspended during the enforced idleness. also for a pro rata part of taxes, insurance and interest on cash value of the plant above described for said time.

Other insurance permitted.

USE AND OCCUPANCY FORM, 300 DAYS.—Fixed Charges.

Adopted January 11, 1906.

See also page 2.
Rate, Building Rate.

$........On the use and occupancy of..................
....................situate................ Chicago, Illinois

The conditions of this contract of insurance are that if the buildings, or any part thereof, or the machinery contained therein, or any part thereof, shall be destroyed, or entirely disabled,

by fire occurring during the term and under the conditions of this policy, so as to entirely prevent operating or carrying on the business, or if the buildings, or any part thereof, or the machinery contained therein, or any part thereof, shall be so damaged or disabled as to partially prevent operating or carrying on the business, then this Company shall be liable for its pro rata part of four-fifths of the loss sustained, ascertained and proven under the conditions of this policy, on account of the following fixed charges, viz., salaries, wages, royalties, taxes, insurance and interest at the lawful rate on the cash value of the plant, for such total or partial prevention not exceeding one-three hundredth (1-300) part of the sum insured under this policy per day for total prevention, nor proportionately for partial prevention, for each working day (of 24 hours) of such total or partial prevention, and for not exceeding three hundred (300) of such working days, nor, in any event, exceeding the sum insured.

Loss, if any, to be computed from the day of the occurrence of any fire to the time when the said buildings and machinery therein could, with ordinary diligence and dispatch, be rebuilt, repaired or replaced, and not limited to the day of expiration named in this policy. For the purposes of this insurance it is agreed that the basis of claim hereunder shall not exceed the legal liability of the assured for salaries and wages of persons employed in connection with the business at the time of the fire, and for royalties not suspended during the enforced idleness, also for a pro rata part of taxes, insurance and interest on cash value of the plant above described for said time.

Other insurance permitted.

USE AND OCCUPANCY FORM.—300 DAYS "MANUFACTURING."

Rate, Building Rate.

Adopted January 11, 1906.

....
$........On the use and occupancy of...................
situate .... Chicago, Illinois.

The conditions of this contract of insurance are that if the buildings, or any part thereof, or the machinery contained therein, or any part thereof, shall be destroyed, or entirely disabled, by fire occurring during the term, and under the conditions of this policy, so as to entirely prevent operating, or carrying on the business, or if the buildings, or any part thereof, or the machinery contained therein, or any part thereof, shall be so damaged or disabled as to prevent the full daily product or output, then this Company shall be liable for its pro rata part of four-fifths of the loss sustained, ascertained and proven under

the conditions of this policy, for such total or partial prevention, not exceeding one-three hundredth (1-300) part of the sum insured under this policy per day for total prevention, nor proportionately, for partial prevention, for each working day (24 hours) of such total or partial prevention, and for not exceeding three hundred (300) of such working days, nor in any event exceeding the sum insured.

Loss, if any, to be computed from the day of the occurrence of any fire to the time when the said buildings and machinery therein could, with ordinary diligence and dispatch, be rebuilt, repaired or replaced, and not limited to the day of expiration named in this policy. For the purpose of this insurance it is agreed that the *net gain from the* total product or output for three hundred (300) working days, beginning with the corresponding day of the year immediately preceding the fire, shall be taken; that the basis of claim for total prevention shall not exceed the daily average of such three hundred (300) days, nor claim for partial prevention a proportionate share of such daily average.

USE AND OCCUPANCY FORM—150 DAYS "MANUFACTURING."

Rate, twice Building Rate.

Adopted January 11, 1906.

$........On the use and occupancy of....................
situate .... Chicago, Illinois.

The conditions of this contract of insurance are that if the buildings, or any part thereof, or the machinery contained therein, or any part thereof, shall be destroyed or entirely disabled, by fire occurring during the term and under the conditions of this policy, so as to entirely prevent operating or carrying on the business, or if the buildings or any part thereof, or the machinery contained therein, or any part thereof, shall be so damaged or disabled, as to prevent the full daily product or output, then this Company shall be liable for its pro rata part of four-fifths of the loss sustained, ascertained and proven under the conditions of this policy, for such total or partial prevention, not exceeding one-one hundred and fiftieth (1-150) part of the sum insured under this policy per day for total prevention, nor proportionately, for partial prevention, for each working day (of 24 hours) of such total or partial prevention, and for not exceeding one hundred and fifty (150) of such working days, nor, in any event, exceeding the sum insured.

Loss, if any, to be computed from the day of the occurrence of any fire to the time when the said buildings and machinery therein could, with ordinary diligence and dispatch, be rebuilt,

repaired or replaced, and not limited to the day of expiration named in this policy. For the purposes of this insurance it is agreed that the *net gain from the* total product or output for one hundred and fifty (150) working days, beginning with the corresponding day of the year immediately preceding the fire, shall be taken; that the basis of claim for total prevention shall not exceed the daily average of such one hundred and fifty (150) days, nor claim for partial prevention a proportionate share of such daily average.

USE AND OCCUPANCY FORM.—300 DAYS OTHER THAN "MANUFACTURING."

Rate, Building Rate.

Adopted January 11, 1906

....

$........On the use and occupancy of.................. situate .... Chicago, Illinois.

The conditions of this contract of insurance are that if the buildings, or any part thereof, or the equipment therein, or any part thereof, shall be destroyed or entirely disabled by fire occurring during the term and under the conditions of this policy, so as to entirely prevent operating, or carrying on the business, or if the buildings, or any part thereof, or the equipment therein, or any part thereof, shall be so damaged or disabled as to prevent the full use or occupancy of the premises, then this Company shall be liable for its pro rata part of four-fifths of the loss sustained, ascertained and proven under the conditions of this policy, for such total or partial prevention, not exceeding one-three hundredth (1-300) part of the sum insured under this policy per day for total prevention, nor proportionately, for partial prevention, for each working day (of 24 hours) of such total or partial prevention, and for not exceeding three hundred (300) of such working days, nor in any event exceeding the sum insured.

Loss, if any, to be computed from the day of the occurrence of any fire to the time when the said building and equipment therein could, with any ordinary diligence and dispatch, be rebuilt, repaired or replaced, and not limited to the day of expiration named in this policy. For the purpose of this insurance it is agreed that the total *net gain* for three hundred (300) working days, beginning with the corresponding day of the year immediately preceding the fire, shall be taken; that the basis of claim for total prevention shall not exceed the daily average of such three hundred (300) days, nor claim for partial prevention a proportionate share of such daily average.

USE AND OCCUPANCY FORM—150 DAYS OTHER THAN "MANUFACTURING."

Rate, twice Building Rate.

Adopted January 11, 1906.

$........On the use and occupancy of..................
situate ....Chicago, Illinois.

The conditions of this contract of insurance are that if the buildings, or any part thereof, or the equipment therein, or any part thereof, shall be destroyed, or entirely disabled, by fire occurring during the term and under the conditions of this policy, so as to entirely prevent operating or carrying on the business, or if the buildings, or any part thereof, or the equipment therein, or any part thereof, shall be so damaged or disabled as to prevent the full use or occupancy of the premises, then this Company shall be liable for its pro rata part of four-fifths of the loss sustained, ascertained and proven under the conditions of this policy, for such total or partial prevention. not exceeding one-one hundred and fiftieth (1-150) part of the sum insured under this policy, per day for total prevention, nor proportionately for partial prevention for each working day (of 24 hours) for such total or partial prevention, and for not exceeding one hundred and fifty (150) of such working days, nor, in any event, exceeding the sum insured.

Loss, if any, to be computed from the day of the occurrence of any fire to the time when the said buildings and equipments therein could, with ordinary diligence and dispatch, be rebuilt. repaired or replaced, and not limited to the day of expiration named in this policy. For the purposes of this insurance it is agreed that the total *net gain* for one hundred and fifty (150) working days, beginning with the corresponding day of the year immediately preceding the fire, shall be taken; that the basis of claim for the total prevention shall not exceed the daily average of such one hundred and fifty (150) days, nor claim for partial prevention a proportionate share of such daily average.

FORM OF BINDER.

Adopted January 11, 1906.

See also page 31.

CHICAGO.............190..

In consideration of the stipulations herein contained, the several insurance companies (each acting and contracting for itself and not one for another) whose names are entered hereon by their respective representatives, together with their signatures as such, are hereby severally bound to....................... as

insurers for.................days, to-wit: from 12 o'clock noon of ....190..until 12 o'clock noon of ....190..against direct loss or damage by fire, to an amount not exceeding the sum set opposite their several names by their respective representatives, to the following described property, while located and contained as described herein, and not elsewhere, to-wit:

....
....
....
....
....
....
....
....
....
....

It is hereby stipulated and agreed that this binder is issued subject to all the terms and conditions of what is commonly known as the Standard Fire Insurance Policy of the State of New York, which are hereby made a part hereof to the same extent as if fully set forth herein; and to the payment of such premiums for the several insurances entered hereon as may be found to be due to the several insurers by their respective representatives, which, in the event of loss before the expiration of this binder, shall be fixed at the full annual premiums for the respective sums insured.

Whenever the policy of any of the insurers is issued in lieu of its undertaking under this binder, its obligation hereunder shall cease and be void.

In no event shall this binder continue in force beyond the time of expiration stated herein.

Name of Insurance Company	Amount Insured in Writing	Amount in Figures	Signatures of Representatives on behalf of Companies

SPECIAL HAZARDS

"No frame or metal clad building occupied in whole or in part for specially hazardous purposes, nor any building occupied for either of the following specially hazardous purposes, viz.:

Agricultural Implement factory.
Bone Black factory.
Brick works.
Breweries.
Butterine factory.
Burial Case or Coffin factory.
Car works.
Carpenter shop (with power).
Carriage or Wagon factory.
Chair factory.
Chemical works.
Cooper shop (with power).
Creosote works.
Currier shops.
Distillery.
Elevator (cleaning, malt or storage).
Felt works.
Fertilizer works.
Floor Cloth or Enameled Cloth factory.
Flour or Feed mill.
Foundry.
Furniture factory.
Gas works.
Glass factory.
Glucose factory.
Glue factory.
Glycerine factory.
Grease rendering or making.
Hominy mill.
Ice House (commercial).
India Rubber Goods factory.
Kindling Wood factory.
Lampblack factory.
Lard Oil refinery.
Lime, Cement or Plaster works.
Linseed Oil mill.
Machine shop.
Malt house.
Match factory.
Morocco factory.
Moulding factory (wood).
Veneer factory.
Vinegar factory.
Wall Paper factory.
White Lead works.
Mustard mill.
Nail factory.
Nut and Bolt works.
Oatmeal mills.
Oil warehouses.
Oil mills.
Oil refineries.
Oilcloth factory.
Oil Clothing factory.
Organ factory.
Paint and Color works.
Paper mills.
Paper Hangings factory.
Patent Leather factory.
Piano factory.
Planing mills.
Plow factory.
Rectifying works (hot process).
Roofing Material factory (asphalt, pitch, etc.).
Sand Paper factory (with dry room).
Sawmills.
Shoddy mills.
Show Case factory (power).
Slaughter houses.
Smoke houses.
Snuff factory.
Soap factory.
Spice mills.
Sporting Goods factory.
Starch factory.
Stave and Heading factory.
Sugar refinery.
Tanneries.
Terra Cotta works.
Tile factory.
Tobacco factory.
Toy factory.
Union Stock Yards—all buildings at.
Varnish factory.
Varnish warehouses.
Woodworking, power (not otherwise named).
Wooden Ware factory.
Wool Pulling.

shall be written for a term exceeding one year, except at pro rata of the annual rates. The Superintendents of Ratings are hereby directed, as new publications of rates are made, to indicate by a letter 'S' on the sheets and cards the risks to which the foregoing rule applies."

"Provided that where the building is under the protection of an automatic sprinkler system, grading seven or better in a scale of ten, it shall be classed as 'ordinary' as to term rate"

MANDATORY TABLE

ums to be charged or Retained for periods less than One Year. Arranged

s.	Per Cent.	Days	Per Cent.	Days.	Per Cent.	Days.	Per Cent.	Days.	Per Ce
	40.33	121	50.33	151	60.33	181	70.17	211	75.1
	40.67	122	50.67	152	60.67	182	70.34	212	75.3
	41.00	123	51.00	153	61.00	183	70.50	213	75.5
	41.33	124	51.33	154	61.33	184	70.67	214	75.6
	41.67	125	51.67	155	61.67	185	70.84	215	75.8
	42.00	126	52.00	156	62.00	186	71.00	216	76.0
	42.33	127	52.33	157	62.33	187	71.17	217	76.1
	42.67	128	52.67	158	62.67	188	71.34	218	76.3
	43.00	129	53.00	159	63.00	189	71.50	219	76.5
	43.33	130	53.33	160	63.33	190	71.67	220	76.6
	43.67	131	53.67	161	63.67	191	71.84	221	76.8
	44.00	132	54.00	162	64.00	192	72.00	222	77.0
	44.33	133	54.33	163	64.33	193	72.17	223	77.1
	44.67	134	54.67	164	64.67	194	72.34	224	77.3
	45.00	135	55.00	165	65.00	195	72.50	225	77.5
	45.33	136	55.33	166	65.33	196	72.67	226	77.6
	45.67	137	55.67	167	65.67	197	72.84	227	77.8
	46.00	138	56.00	168	66.00	198	73.00	228	78.0
	46.33	139	56.33	169	66.33	199	73.17	229	78.1
	46.67	140	56.67	170	66.67	200	73.34	230	78.3
	47.00	141	57.00	171	67.00	201	73.50	231	78.5
	47.33	142	57.33	172	67.33	202	73.67	232	78.6
	47.67	143	57.67	173	67.67	203	73.84	233	78.8
	48.00	144	58.00	174	68.00	204	74.00	234	79.0

Auditor of current bills............................... 20
Of accounts of corporation...................... 20

by days from One to Three Hundred and Sixty Days,

nt.	Days.	Per Cent.	Days.	Per Cent.	Days	Per Cent.	Days.	Per Cent.
7	241	80.17	271	85.17	301	90.17	331	95.17
4	242	80.34	272	85.34	302	90.34	332	95.34
0	243	80.50	273	85.50	303	90.50	333	95.50
7	244	80.67	274	85.67	304	90.67	334	95.67
4	245	80.84	275	85.84	305	90.84	335	95.84
	246	81.00	276	86.00	306	91.00	336	96.00
7	247	81.17	277	86.17	307	91.17	337	96.17
4	248	81.34	278	86.34	308	91.34	338	96.34
	249	81.50	279	86.50	309	91.50	339	96.50
7	250	81.67	280	86.67	310	91.67	340	96.67
4	251	81.84	281	86.84	311	91.84	341	96.84
	252	82.00	282	87.00	312	92.00	342	97.00
7	253	82.17	283	87.17	313	92.17	343	97.17
4	254	82.34	284	87.34	314	92.34	344	97.34
	255	82.50	285	87.50	315	92.50	345	97.50
7	256	82.67	286	87.67	316	92.67	346	97.67
	257	82.84	287	87.84	317	92.84	347	97.84
	258	83.00	288	88.00	318	93.00	348	98.00
7	259	83.17	289	88.17	319	93.17	349	98.17
	260	83.34	290	88.34	320	93.34	350	98.34
	261	83.50	291	88.50	321	93.50	351	98.50
7	262	83.67	292	38.67	322	93.67	352	98.67
	263	83.84	293	88.84	323	93.84	353	98.84
	264	84.00	294	89.00	324	94.00	354	99.00

INDEX

	PAGE
Accounts of the corporation	16
Fire patrol	16
Of funds of patrol	20
Acetylene Gas, rule regarding	30
Form of permit for	60
Act to incorporate The Chicago Board of Underwriters	1
Additional Premiums, rule regarding	30
Adjustment Clause, rule regarding	30
Advance information, misstatements regarding	22
Regarding rates	21
Advance charges of railroads and transportation companies, writing of without co-insurance	24
Affairs outside of Cook County, bureau on	20
Affairs of the corporation, management of	19
Agent of the corporation	26
Agents of fire insurance companies, eligibility of to membership in class one	11
Agreed percentages of contribution	23
Air Pressure Lamps using gasoline, form of permit for	75
Amendments to the Constitution	17
Animals, insurance of	39, 43
Annual Meeting	13
Apartment Buildings, rating of and application of co-insurance to	24
Apartment houses in certain districts	46, 53
Definition of	47, 53, 59
Appeal Committee, powers and duties of	20
Appeal from finding of committee on fines and penalities	27
Appeal from ruling of Executive Committee	19
Appeal and arbitration committee	15
Applications for rates	22
Arbitration and Appeal Committee, members of	15
Armstrong, E. A. Mfg. Co., form of floater for	61
Arson, discovery and punishment of	9
Assessments, payment of by members	41
Fixing amount of	20
Payment of by persons withdrawing from membership	17
For expenses of corporation	16
For support of fire patrol	16
Collection of by Secretary	18
Assignments, rule regarding	30, 37, 38
Attics	46, 47, 52, 55
Auditor of current bills	20
Of accounts of corporation	20

	PAGE
Authority of sub-committees	16
Automobiles, rule regarding	30
Using gasoline, form of permit for	63, 64, 65
Form of floater for electric	62, 63
Average Clause, use of	30, 32, 42
Form of	65
In connection with blanket insurance on certain property	32
Use of in connection with 100 per cent clause	32
Average rates	21
Revision of annually	21
Supervision of	21
Bags and Bagging, form of floater for	66
Bank in which to deposit funds	18
Benzine, etc., rule regarding	31
Form for use of	75, 76, 77
Binders, issuance of	22
Rule regarding	31
Form for	117
Blanket insurance on buildings insured with other items	23
Blanket Insurance, rule regarding	32
Board of Trustees of Patrolmen's Pension Fund	16
Boarding Houses (private) rates on	22
Boiler and engine, insurance of	39, 42
Bond of the Secretary	19
Bond of Treasurer	18
Books of account, keeping of	18
Breaches of by-laws, etc	20
Breweries, application of consequential damage to	35
Rule regarding insurance of	32, 42
Brick Buildings and contents occupied for apartment house or flats, in a certain location	46, 53
Brick Veneered, exposure by	49, 56
Brokerages	24
Rule regarding	32
Brokerage, date from which paid	25
Brokerage on preferred or sprinklered risks placed under certain conditions	21
Buildings not in process of construction, not rated	47, 48, 55, 57
Buildings part brick and part frame, exposure by	49, 56
Building Insurance, deduction in rate for use of 100 per cent contribution	23
Buildings, brick, in section 2 outside district	56
One story, etc., writing of without co-insurance	24
Allowance for superior construction of	21
Buildings insured with other subjects under general or blanket forms, with 90 per cent or 100 per cent contribution, allowance for	23
Building Insurance, deduction in rate for use of 90 per cent contribution	23
Rule regarding	32

PAGE

Buildings of dwelling construction used for manufacturing or
    mercantile purposes 32, 46, 52
Buildings in process of construction, rule regarding....33, 47, 54
Buildings unoccupied, insurance of....................... 32
Buildings unrated, occupied for manufacturing or mechan-
    ical work 40
Buildings or sub-divisions thereof, etc., insurance of......32, 42
Building Equipment Floater, form of...................... 66
Building Non-Occupancy Clause, form of.................. 67
Buildings, frame commercial and contents, rates on........ 57
Bureau on affairs outside of Cook County.................. 20
By-laws 1, 18
    Provision for 17
    Powers of 17
    Observance of by members 13
    Construction of provisions of........................ 19
    Amendment to 29
    Investigation of breaches of.......................... 26
Calcium Carbide, rule regarding.........................30, 33
    Permit for storage of 67
Cancelled policies, allowance of rebates on................. 22
Cancellations, rule regarding.............................. 34
Cancellation of insurance covering in elevators............. 37
Cartage, insurance of 43
Central Office District, boundaries of..................... 10
Chairman of Executive Committee........................ 15
Chairman of Patrol Committee, duties of regarding Patrol-
    men's Pension Fund 16
Change in construction 22
Change in occupancy 22
Change in ownership 22
Change in risk, rule regarding............................. 34
Charitable Institutions, rate on............................ 22
Checks, issuing and signing of............................ 18
Chicago Board of Underwriters, law authorizing incorpora-
    tion of 1
Chicago Embroidering and Braiding Co., form of floater for 68
Chicago Law Institute, form of floater for.................. 69
Chief Surveyor, nominations for 14
    Election of 14
    Term of office of.................................... 14
    Successor to 14
    Deputy to 14
    Removal of 19
    Duties of 19
Churches 48, 53
    Rates on 22
Class Five, brokerage to.................................. 25
    Standard of eligibility for members of................ 12
    Representation of companies by members of.......... 12
    Payment of dues by 12

	PAGE
Withdrawal of members of	17
Class Four, standard of eligibility for membership in	12
Withdrawal of members of	17
Business and office of	12
Payment of dues by	12
Representation of companies by members of	12
Brokerage to	25
Class One, standard of eligibility to membership in	1
Withdrawal of members of	17
Brokerage between members of	24
Class of Offense against rules	20
Class Three, representation of companies by members of	12
Payment of dues by	12
Office and business of	12
Standard of eligibility for membership in	12
Withdrawal of members of	17
Brokerage on business placed with members	25
Class Two, standard of eligibility to membership in	11
Withdrawal of members of	17
Publication of rates in district one to	21
Brokerage on business placed by with members of class one	25
Brokerage on business placed with members of class two	25
Classification Committee, power given to regarding certain forms of permits	31
Powers and duties of	21
Members of	15
Changing of	21
Classification of risks as to term rate	34
Club Houses, rates on	22
Coal Sheds, rule regarding	34, 42
Insurance of	42
Coal Yards	48, 53
Co-insurance on certain property	23, 24
Commercial Building, definition of	39
Commercial Building Form	39, 69
Commercial Buildings (frame)	48, 55
Commercial, frame buildings, and contents, rates on	57
Commission, allowance to certain persons	25
Date from which paid	25
To solicitors and office employes	26
To non-members or suspended members	26
Commissions	24
Insurance of	35, 41
Commission and profits, insurance on	35, 41
Committees, powers and duties	19
Record of proceedings of	18
On Arbitration and Appeal	15
On classifications, powers and duties of	21
On classifications, rates and schedules	15

	PAGE
Classifications of hazards	15
(Sub) appointment of	15
Authority of	16
(Sub) vacancies on	16
(Special) appointment of	15
Provision for in charter	2
Vacancies on	16
Election of	14
Committees on Fines and Penalties, appointment of	15
Common Carrier's Liability, rule regarding	35, 41
Insurance of	35, 41
Company representation, rule regarding	11
Members of classes Three, Four and Five	12
Compressed Air House Cleaning Machines, form of floater for	70
Condition of risks within jurisdiction of corporation	19
Consent to assignment by endorsement	31, 38
Consequential Damage Clause, form of permit for	70, 71
Consequential Damage, rule regarding	35
Application of to breweries	35
Insurance of	35, 41
Consolidation of returns of premiums	16
Constitution of The Chicago Board of Underwriters	9, 10, 11, 12, 13, 14, 15, 16, 17
Observance of by members	13
Amendments to	17
Construction of provisions of	19
Constitution and By-laws	1
Construction of provisions of Constitution, etc	19
Construction, change in	22, 34
Contents of certain properties, average rates on	21
Contents Insurance	36, 42
In district No. 2	55, 57
Contractor's Floater, form of	72
Contribution	23
Contribution Clause, form of	73
Contributors to fire patrol, meeting of	3
Cook County, division of into districts	10
Representation of companies	11
Corporation, expenses of	16
Provision of power of	2
Corporate name of	9
Record of proceedings of meetings of	18
Corporation affairs, management of	19
Counsel, professional, employment of by members relative to discipline	28
County District, boundaries of	10
Crude Petroleum, rule regarding	37
Form for use of	73
Crude Petroleum Permit, form of	73
Cyclone Insurance	49, 54

	PAGE
Current Expenses, definition of	20
Decorations of a building, rate on	32, 42
Delinquents	26
Deputies to the Manager, Secretary, Superintendents of Ratings or Chief Surveyor	14
Devices using gasoline, etc., rule regarding	31, 40
Discipline	26
Disregard of obligations	17
Districts in which members may transact business	10
Dues, expenditure of money received from	16
Payment of by members of classes Three, Four and Five	12
Payment of by persons withdrawing from membership	17
Separate account of	16
Duties of classification committee	21
Of committees	19
Of Committee on Fines and Penalties	20
Of Patrol Committee	20
Of President	18
Of Vice-President	18
Of Treasurer	18
Of Manager	18
Of Secretary	18
Of Chief Surveyor	19
Of Superintendents of Ratings	19
Duties and powers of Committee on Arbitration and Appeal	20
Dwellings, definition of	47, 53
Rates on	22
Dwellings used for mercantile or manufacturing purposes	32, 46, 52
Dwellings and contents, writing of without co-insurance	23
Dynamos, insurance of	37, 42
Elections	14
Election of committees	14
Election of Patrol Committee	15
Electric Current Clause, form of	74
Electrical Apparatus Floater, form of	74
Electrical Apparatus, insuring of	36, 37
Electrical Exemption Clause, form of	74
Electric Light and Power Generating Plants	37, 42
Electric Light Plants and other electrical apparatus, insuring of with furniture and fixtures	36
Elevators, insurance of	37, 42
Transfer of Insurance in	37
Assignment of policies covering in	30
Form of floater for	66
Cancellation of insurance in	34
Elevators (grain) form for insurance of storage charges in	101
Average rates on	21
Elevator and Warehouse Insurance, application of average clause to	31

	PAGE
Eligibility, standard for by members of classes Three, Four and Five	12
Of persons to membership	10
Of solicitors	25
Employes of Corporation	18
Endorsements, rule regarding	30, 31, 38
Errors relative to discipline	27
Excess Insurance, rule regarding	38
Executive Committee, election of members of	14
Chairman of	15
Appeal from rulings of	19
Powers and duties of	19
Meetings of	19
Rules governing	19
Record of proceedings of	20
Report by	20
Election of	14
Term of	15
Existing rates binding	22
Expenditures of corporation, supervision of by Executive Committee	20
Expenditure of moneys received from dues, fees and fines	16
Expenses of the corporation, contribution toward	16
Current, definition of	20
Expenses of fire patrol, amount of	3
Expenses in underwriting, discouragement of extravagant	9
Expired Policies, rebate on	22
Farm Property, rates on	58
Definition of	58
Fees, expenditure of moneys received from	16
For registering Solicitors and clerks	26
Separate account of	16
Fifty per cent contribution, charge for	23
Fines assessed against members	27
Authority for in charter	2
For violations of rules	20
Expenditure of moneys received from	16
Separate account of	16
Fines and Penalties Committee, appeal from decision of	27
Method of procedure by	28
Powers and duties of	20
Committee on	15
Fire Insurance Companies, eligibility of officers of to membership	11
Eligibility of agents of to membership in class One	11
Representation of in Cook County	11
Fire losses, distribution of	9
Fire Maps, use of in making minimum rates	22
Fire Patrol, expenses of	3
Meeting of contributors to	3
Accommodations and apparatus for	3

	PAGE
Expenses of	16
Law enabling boards to maintain	3
Fire protection, maintenance of system of	9
Fire Wardens, provision for in charter	2
Fire works	38
Five per cent exception clause, use of	32
Flats, rates on	22
Definition of	59
Flats and contents, writing of without co-insurance	23
Flats or apartment houses in certain districts	46, 53
Definition of	47, 53
Rating of and application of co-insurance to	24
Floaters, forms of for	
E. A. Armstrong Mfg. Co.	61
Electric automobiles	62, 63
Automobiles using gasoline	64, 65
Bags and Bagging	66
Building Equipment	66
Chicago Embroidering and Braiding Co.	68
Chicago Law Institute	69
Compressed air house cleaning machines	70
Contractors	72
Electrical apparatus	74
Hastings Express Co.	78, 79, 80
House furnishings and decorations in private residences	80
Household furniture	82
Lincoln Warehouse & Van Co.	84
Retail meat market	85
Merchandise in cars on track	86
Merchandise in cars on track in U. S. Yards	86
General merchandise	87
Machinery, wood and metal working	88
Mutoscope Company	90
Paper hangers', painters' and decorators' tools and implements	93
Patterns	94
Piano and organ	94, 95
Pawnbrokers	96
Property upon which the assured may loan money	96
Regalia and paraphernalia	96
Saloon and furniture and fixtures	100
Tailors	102
Teaming outfit	103
Merchandise in hands of teamsters	103
Railroad and steamboat warehouse	104, 105, 106, 107
Railroad ties and telegraph poles	108
Soda fountains	109
Streets Western Stable Car Line	110
Thomson and Taylor Spice Co.	111
Transmitting typewriters	112
Floating policies	38

	PAGE
Form, substitution or modification of by endorsement	31, 38
Forms	39, 60
Forms for Acetylene Gas	60
E. A. Armstrong Mfg. Co.	61
Electric automobiles	62, 63
Automobiles using gasoline	63, 64, 65
Average Clauses	65
Bags and Bagging Floater	66
Building Equipment (elevators)	66
Building non-occupancy clause	67
Binders	117
Calcium Carbide	67
Chicago Embroidering and Braiding Co.	68
Chicago Law Institute	69
Commercial Building Form	69
Compressed air house cleaning machines	70
Consequential Damage Clause	70, 71
Contractors Floater	72
Contribution Clause	73
Item Contribution Clause	73
Crude Petroleum Permit	73
Electrical Apparatus floater	74
Electric Current Clause	74
Electrical exemption clause	74
Gasoline Engine Permit	75
Gasoline for lighting in air pressure lamps	75
Gasoline for lighting in gravity lamps	76
Gasoline for lighting in oil distribution system	76
Gasoline stove permit	77
Hasting Express Co. floaters	78, 79, 80
House furnishings and decorations floater in private residences	80
Household furniture floater	82
Lightning Clause	83
Limited loss claim form—buildings fireproof construction	83
Lincoln Warehouse and Van Co.	84
Loss Payable Clause	84
Lumber Exclusion Clause	85
Lumber Vacancy Clause	85
Meat Market (retail)	85
Merchandise in cars on track	86
Merchandise in cars on track in U. S. Yards	86
Merchandise (general)	87
Machinery, wood and metal working	88
Mortgage Clause	88
Mortgage Clause with full contribution	89
Mutoscope Company	90
Occupancy Clause	91
Permit for openings in party walls with standard iron doors	91

	PAGE
Specifications for standard iron doors	92
Permit for openings in party walls with vault iron doors	92
Specifications for vault iron doors	93
Paper hangers', painters' and decorators' tools and implements floater	93
Patterns (general) floater	94
Piano and organ floater	94, 95
Printers' Benzine Warranty	56
Property upon which the assured may loan money	96
Regalia and paraphernalia floater	96
Removal permit	96
Insurance on rents	97, 98
Insurance of rental values	97, 98
Safes and Vaults	99
Saloon furniture and fixtures	100
Storage charges in grain elevators and storage warehouses	101
Tailors floating policy	102
Tailors Merchandise policy	102
Teaming outfit floater	103
Merchandise in hands of teamsters	103
Railroad and Steamboat Warehouse Floater	104, 105
Railroad and Steamboat Warehouse Metal Floater	106, 107
Railroad ties and telegraph poles	108
Soda fountains	109
Sprinkler Maintenance Clause	110
Streets Western Stable Car Line	110
Thomson & Taylor Spice Co	111
Transmitting typewriters	112
Use and occupancy	113, 114, 115, 116, 117
Foundations, insurance of	33
Frame Commercial Buildings and contents	48, 55, 57
Freight advances, insurance of	43
Funds, depository for	18
Funds of Fire Patrol, expenditure of	16
Separate account of	16
Funds for maintenance of patrol	20
Funds received from dues, fees and fines, account and expenditures of	16
Furniture and fixtures, insurance of	36, 42
Gasoline, rule regarding	31
Form for use of	75, 76, 77
Gasoline Engine Permit, form of	75
Gasoline Lamps, form of permit for	75, 76
Gasoline Stove Permit, form of	77
Government, limit of	9
Grain, insurance of	42
Grain elevators, insurance on	37
Specific average rates on	21
Form for insurance of storage charges in	101

	PAGE
Grain storage warehouse, insurance of	37
Gravity Lamps, form of permit for use of	76
Halls without scenery	22
Hastings Express Co. Floater, form of	78, 79, 80
Hazard, change in	34
Notification of company of increase in	34
House Cleaning Machines, form of floater for	70
House Furnishings and Decorations Floater, form of	80
Household Furniture Floater, form of	82
Household furniture, writing of without co-insurance	24
Improvements in a risk at the expense of members	41
Improvements and decorations, rate on	32, 42
Ineligibility of members of any class	12
Increase in hazard, notification to company regarding	34
Information (advance) misstatements regarding	22
Regarding rates	21
Inspections, record of all made	19
Publication of to members	19
Making of	19
Inspection, maintenance of system of	9
Insurance written for less than a term, rates on	23
Insurance without co-insurance	23
Insurance on unrated risks	40
Insurance written blanket, rule regarding	32
Invalidation of policy by the act of another committed without the knowledge of the assured	34
Investigation of breaches of by-laws, etc.	20
Iron doors, standard	91, 92
Iron storage tanks, insuring of blanket	32
Item Contribution Clause, form of	73
Leasehold Interests, insurance of	35, 39, 41
Liability of railroad and transportation companies as common carriers, the advance charges of same, writing of without co-insurance	24
Lightning Clause, form of	83
Limit of Government	9
Limited Loss Claim Form, buildings of fireproof construction	83
Lincoln Warehouse and Van Floater, form of	84
Livery, boarding, sale and team stables	39, 43, 46, 52
Loss Claim form, limited, buildings of fireproof construction	83
Loss payable clause	38, 44, 84
Form of	84
Losses by fire, distribution of	9
Lumber, insurance of	39, 42
Lumber Exclusion Clause, form of	85
Lumber Vacancy Clause, form of	85
Lumber yards	48, 53
Machinery, hoisting, in coal sheds	34
Machinery, insurance of with building	39, 42
Machinery, wood and metal working floater, form of	88

	PAGE
Machinery or apparatus used in manufacturing, Insurance of with building	33, 42
Machinery pertaining to the service of the building, insurance of with building	33
Malt Elevators, insurance of	37
Malt Houses, insurance of	39, 42
Manager, chairman of Executive Committee	15
Deputy to	14
Removal of	18
Term of office of	14
Successor to	14
Duties of	18
Powers of	18
Nominations for	14
Election of	14
Manufactories, insurance of	39, 42
Manufacturing business in dwellings	32
Manufacturing or mechanical work in premises unrated	40
Manufacturing machinery or apparatus, insuring of with building	33
Maps, fire, use of in making minimum rates	22
Materials and articles, use of	40
Matters not provided for in Constitution and By-laws, rules governing	17
Meat Market (retail) form of floater for	85
Meetings	13
Meetings of the Corporation and standing committees, record of	18
Meetings of contributors to fire patrol	3
Members suspended, dealing with	26
Commission to	26
Members of all classes, ineligibility of	12
Members withdrawing from membership, payment of dues and assessments by	17
Members not having power to vote	13
Members' responsibility for acts of employes and solicitors	25
Memberships, definition of	10
Qualifications to	10
Privileges of	10
Membership Agreement	13
Membership in class Five, standard of	12
Membership in class Four, standard of eligibility for	12
Membership in class One	10, 11
Membership in class Three, standard of eligibility	12
Membership in class No. Two, standard of eligibility for	11
Membership of new partners in firms	12
Mercantile or manufacturing business in dwellings	32, 46, 52
Mercantile Buildings, insurance of contents of for longer than one year	50
Merchandise, insurance	35, 42, 50, 59
Merchandise (general) floater, form of	87

PAGE

Merchandise in cars on tracks, form of floater for.......... 86
Merchandise in hands of teamsters, form of floater for...... 103
Merchandise in cars on tracks in U. S. Yards, form of floater
  for 86
Merchandise contained in a storage warehouse storing to-
  bacco, rate on 36, 42
Merchandise insurance including commission and profits.... 35
Metal working machinery, form of floater for.............. 88
Metals in ingots and pigs and scrap metal.................. 36
Mills and manufactories, insurance of.................... 39, 42
Minimum rates.. 22
Minimum Tariff, application of............................ 22
  For inside district................................. 45
  Outside district 51
  Questions arising relative to application of........ 22
Minutes of proceedings of Executive Committee............ 20
  Standing committees and corporation............... 18
Misstatements regarding rates............................. 22
Money received from dues, fees and fines, expenditure and
  separate account of............................ 16
  Collected by Secretary, disposition of.............. 18
  Disbursed, orders for.............................. 19
  Expenditure of certain amount of................... 19
Mortgage Clause, form of................................. 88
  With full contribution, form of..................... 88
Motors, insurance of..................................... 42
Mutoscope Company floater, form of...................... 90
Mutual Plan of Policy.................................... 22
Naphtha, rule regarding use of............................ 31
  Form for use of 75, 76, 77
Ninety per cent contribution, deduction for................ 23
Nominations for members of Executive Committee.......... 14
  For members of Patrol Committee................... 15
  The office of Manager, Executive Committee, Secre-
   tary, Superintendents of Ratings, Chief Survey-
   or, making of............................... 14
Non-members, dealing with............................... 26
  Commission to 26
Non-Occupancy Clause, form of........................... 67
Non-voting members 13
Notice of reduction in rates............................... 21
Notice of withdrawal of members......................... 17
Object of the corporation 29
Obligations, disregard of................................. 17
Observance of the rules of the corporation................ 11
Occupancy, rule regarding 33, 40
  Form for 91
Occupancy Clause, form of............................... 91
Occupancy of buildings in process of construction........... 33
Occupancy, change in 22, 34
Offenses against rules.................................... 20

	PAGE
Office (principal) of the corporation	9
Officers	2, 14
Officers of companies, eligibility of to membership	11
Offices, rates on	22
Offices of members of the corporation	11
Offices of members of class Five	12
Offices of members of class Four	12
Offices of members class Three	12
Offices of members of class No. Two	11
Oil Distribution System, form of permit for	76
One hundred per cent, deduction in rate for	23
Open Entries	40
Open Insurance	40
Openings in party walls with vault iron doors	92
Openings in party walls, form of permit for with standard iron doors	91
Openings in walls	34
Orders on Treasurer for moneys disbursed	19
Ordinary class of property relative to commission	24
Outbuildings	46, 52
Outbuildings on rear of adjoining lots or on same premises, exposure of	49
Ownership, change in	22
Packing house products, property used for the manufacture and storage of, average rates on	21
Paper hangers', painters' and decorators' tools and implements, form of floater for	93
Partners, admission of to firms already members	12
Patent Devices	40
Patrol (fire) meeting of contributors to	3
Expenses of	3
Accommodations and apparatus for	3
Law enabling boards to maintain	3
Expenses of	16
Patrol Committee, election of members of	14
Term of members of	15
Nominations for members of	15
Powers and duties of	20
Election of	15
Patrolmen, law providing for the pensioning of	5
Law providing for the pensioning of widows and children of	5, 6, 7, 8
Patrolmen's Pension Fund, law authorizing	5, 6, 7, 8
Maintenance of	16
Patterns (general) floater, form of	94
Pawnbrokers floating policy	96
Penalties Committee, powers and duties of	20
Penalties and Fines Committee appointment of	15
Pension Fund, maintenance of	9
Law authorizing	5, 6, 7, 8
Maintenance of	9

PAGE

Percentages of contribution.................................... 23
Permission for use of premises............................. 40
Permits, forms of for
    Acetylene Gas 60
    Automobiles using gasoline 63
    Storage of calcium carbide............................ 67
    Crude petroleum 73
    Gasoline engine 75
    Use of gasoline for lighting in air pressure lamps ... 75
    Use of gasoline for lighting in gravity lamps........ 76
    Gasoline for lighting in oil distribution system........ 76
    Gasoline stove 77
    Openings in party walls............................91, 92
Petroleum (crude) Permit, form of....................... 73
    Crude, permission for use of......................... 37
    Form for use of 73
    Light products of, permits for........................ 31
Piano and Organ Floater, form of........................94, 95
Policy, reduction of money paid for........................ 22
Policies cancelled or expired, cancellation of................ 22
Policies invalidation of... 34
Policies issued on the mutual plan.......................... 22
Power Generating Plants.................................37, 42
Powers of the corporation 2, 9
Powers of Manager.. 18
Power to vote... 13
Powers and duties of classification committee.............. 21
Powers and duties of committees.......................... 19
Powers and duties of Committee on Arbitration and Appeal 20
Powers and duties of Committee on Fines and Penalties.... 20
Powers and duties of Patrol Committee..................... 20
Preferred business, placing of under certain conditions...... 21
    Rates on 21
Preferred class of property relating to commissions........ 24
Premises, permission for use of.............................. 40
Premiums, additional, rule regarding....................... 30
    Return of for support of fire patrol.................. 16
    Publication of amount returned by members.......... 16
    Return of for expenses of corporation and patrol.... 16
    Consolidation of 16
    Received in the city of Chicago, statement of 3, 4
    Publication of amount reported for fire patrol........ 16
President, election of.. 14
    Duties of regarding Patrolmen's Pension Fund...... 16
    Member of Executive Committee 15
    Term of office of... 14
    Successor to.. 14
    Duties 18
Principal office of the corporation........................... 9
Principal city district, boundaries of........................ 10
Printers' Benzine Warranty, form of....................... 96

	PAGE
Private barns and outbuildings on rear of same premises, exposure by	49
Private Boarding Houses, rates on	22
Private mark on surveys	21
Private stables, rates on	22
Privileges of memberships	10
Profits, insurance on	35-41
Promulgation of rates	19
Promulgation of special rates on sprinklered or preferred risks and method of placing same	21
Promulgation of specific rates	21
Promulgated rate binding	23
Property located in district No. One, promulgation of rates on to members of class Two	21
Property of Board in hands of persons withdrawing from membership	17
Property south of Harrison St., minimum rates on	22
Property upon which the assured may loan money, form of floater for	96
Pro rata cancellations	34
Proxies	13
Public Institutions, rates on	22
Publication of returns made by members	16
Publication of withdrawal of members	17
Punishment for mis-statements regarding advance information	22
Quarterly meeting	13
Questions arising relative to application of minimum rates	22
Quorum	13
Railroad and Steamboat Warehouse floater—	
Limited form of	104
Unlimited	105
Railroad and Steamboat Warehouse metal floater—	
Limited form for	106
Unlimited form for	107
Railroad and Transportation Company, liability of as common carriers, the advance charges of same, writing of without co-insurance	24
Railroad ties and telegraph poles floater, form of	108
Rate reductions by other than schedules	22, 41
Rates, consideration of reduction in	21
Application for specific	22
Committee on	15
Observance of by members	13
(Average) supervision of	21
Change in by reason of certain changes in risk	22
Not fixed by schedule, supervision of	21
On preferred risks	21
(Specific) making of	21
On sprinklered risks	21
Promulgated binding	23

	PAGE
Reduction of in open meeting	22
Correct copies of all made	19
Promulgation of	19
Violation of and investigation of breaches of	26
Binding on members	22
Rates in district No. One, publication of to members of class No. Two	21
Rating of risks within the jurisdiction of corporation	19
Rebate on endorsement	31-38
Rebates	22
Rebates on a cancelled policy	22
Receipts for moneys received	18
Record, publication of	20-28
Failure to reply to	29
Reduction in rates, consideration of	21
In open meeting	22
Regalia and paraphernalia Floater, form for	96
Regulations, observance of by members	13
Reinsurance rule	41
Removal permit	97
Rental Values, form No. 1 for insurance of	97
Form No. 2 for insurance of	98
Insurance of	41
Rents, form No. 1 for insurance of	98
Form No. 2 for insurance of	99
Rents and rental values, insurance of	41
Report of Executive Committee	20
Responsibility of members employing solicitors	25
Returns of premiums for expense of corporation and Patrol	16
Returns of premiums for expenses of fire patrol, publication of	16
Returns and Assessments, rule regarding	41
Return of premiums, publication of	16
Revenue, fixing amount of	16-20
Revision of schedules	21
Reward to be paid informers relative to discipline	28
Risks within the jurisdiction of the corporation rating of	19
Condition of	19
Rules	30
Violation of and investigation of breaches	26
Observance of	11, 13
Construction of	19
Provision for	17
Making of in open meeting	17
Safes and Vaults, property in	41
Form for insuring property in	99
Saloon furniture and fixture floater	100
Schedules, revision of	21
Adoption of	21
Preparation of new	21
Committee on	15

	PAGE
Schedules and tariffs, application of	19
Schools, rates on	22
School Houses	48-53
Secretary, bond of	19
Removal of	19
Duties of regarding Patrolmen's Pension Fund	15
Election of	14
Deputy to	14
Term of office of	14
Successor to	14
Duties of	18
Nominations for	14
Separate accounts of funds of fire patrol	16
Separate subjects of insurance	41
Separate subjects of insurance written blanket	32
Seventy per cent contribution, addition for	23
Short rate cancellations	34
Short rates	23
Short rate table	121-122
Short term insurance	23
Sixty per cent contribution, addition for	23
Soda Fountains, form of floater for	109
Solicitors	25
Special Committees, appointment of	15
Special Hazards written for a term, list of	119
Special meetings	13
Specific rates, making of	21
Application for	22
Promulgation of	21
Reduction of in open meetings	22
Specifications for standard iron doors	92
Specifications for vault iron doors	93
Sprinklered business, placing of under certain conditions	21
Sprinklered risks—maintenance clause	43
Rates on	21
Sprinkler Leakage, insurance of	41
Sprinkler Maintenance Clause, form for	110
Stables (private), rates on	22
Stables, private, and contents, writing of without co-insurance	24
Stables, livery, boarding and sales	39, 43, 46, 52, 53
Stables and Outbuildings	46, 52
Standard iron doors	91, 92
Standing Committees, records of	18
Stipulations on a policy affecting rebate	22
Storage Charges, in grain elevators and storage warehouses, form for	101
Insurance of	43, 41
Form for	101
Insurance of	41
Storage Tanks, iron, insuring of blanket	32

	PAGE
Storage Warehouses, assignment of policies covering in	30
Average rates on	21
Application of average clause to	31
Cancellation of insurance in	34
Form for insurance of storage charges in	101
Store furniture and fixtures, insurance of	36, 42
Stores and Apartment Houses, definition of	59
Stores and flats, etc, without co-insurance	24
Definition of	59
Streets not considered as exposures	46, 52
Streets Western Stable Car Line, form of floater for	110
Sub-committees, appointment of	15
Vacancies on	16
Sub-division (territorial) of Cook County	10
Substitution or modification of form by endorsement	31, 38
Suburban City District, boundaries of	10
Superintendents of Ratings, nominations for	14
Term of office of	14
Successor to	14
Deputy to	14
Election of	14
Duties of	19
Removal of	19
Superior Construction of buildings, allowance for	21
Surplus insurance	26
Surveyor (chief), election of	14
Term of office of	14
Successor to	14
Deputy to	14
Nominations for	14
Removal of	19
Duties of	19
Surveyors and Fire Wardens, provision for in charter	2
Surveys, making of	19
Private mark on regarding rates	21
Suspended members, dealing with	26
Commission to	26
Switchboards, insurance of	42
Tailors' floating policy, form for	102
Tailors' Merchandise policy, form for	102
Tanks, iron storage, insuring of blanket	32
Tariffs, observance of by members	13
Violation and investigation of breaches of	26
Application of	19
Teaming outfit floater, form for	103
Teaming Stables	39, 43, 46, 52, 53
Definition of	39
Term of committees	15
Term of employment of solicitors	26
Term of officers	14
Term of members of Patrol Committee	15

	PAGE
Term insurance on buildings in process of construction	33
Term Rates on certain property	50, 58
Term rates on certain risks	34
Territorial subdivisions of Cook County	10
Thomson and Taylor Spice Co., form of floater for	111
Three agency rule	11
Title of the corporation	9
Tobacco, insurance of	36, 42
Tornado insurance	42, 49, 54
Tornado and Cyclone Insurance	49, 54
Transfer by endorsement	31, 38
Transfer of insurance	43
Transmitting Typewriters—form of floater for	112
Transportation companies and railroads, liability of as common carriers, the advance charges of same, writing of without co-insurance	24
Treasurer, bond of	18
Duties of	18
Term of office of	14
Successor to	14
Duties of regarding Patrolmen's Pension Fund	16
Election of	14
Trial of members violating rules, etc.	27
Trustees of Patrolmen's Pension Fund	16
Underwriting, encouragement of good practices in	9
Union Stock Yards district, average rates on property in	21
Unoccupied buildings, rule regarding	32
Use and Occupancy Insurance	42
Forms for	113, 114, 115, 116, 117
Vacancies, elections to fill	14
Vacancies on committees	16
Values, statement of, revision of annually	21
Vault iron doors	92, 93
Vaults, form for insuring property in	99
Vaults and safes, property in	41
Form for	99
Vessels laid up, writing of without co-insurance	24
Vice President, duties of	18
Election of	14
Member of Executive Committee	15
Term of office of	14
Successor to	14
Vote, power to	13
Vote on reduction of rates	23
Vote required to admit applicants to membership in class No. One	11
Vote required to admit new partners to membership in the corporation	12
Voting through the Record	17
Voting in writing	17
Voting by proxy	13

	PAGE
Vouchers for expenditures by patrol committee	20
Taking of for all disbursements	18
Waiver of right of subrogation	44
Warehouse, public storage, cancellation of insurance in	34
Warehouse Insurance	44
Application of average clause to	31
Warehouses (storage), form for insurance of storage charges in	101
Assignment of policies covering in	30
Application of average clause to	31
Average rates on	21
Wilful offense relating to discipline	27
Wiring and connections, insurance of	42
Withdrawals of members other than members of class One	17
Definition of	17
From membership	17
Wood and Metal working machinery, form of floater for	88
Wood working risks in process of construction	48, 53

CPSIA information can be obtained
at www.ICGtesting.com
Printed in the USA
BVHW091242021118
531988BV00012B/1255/P